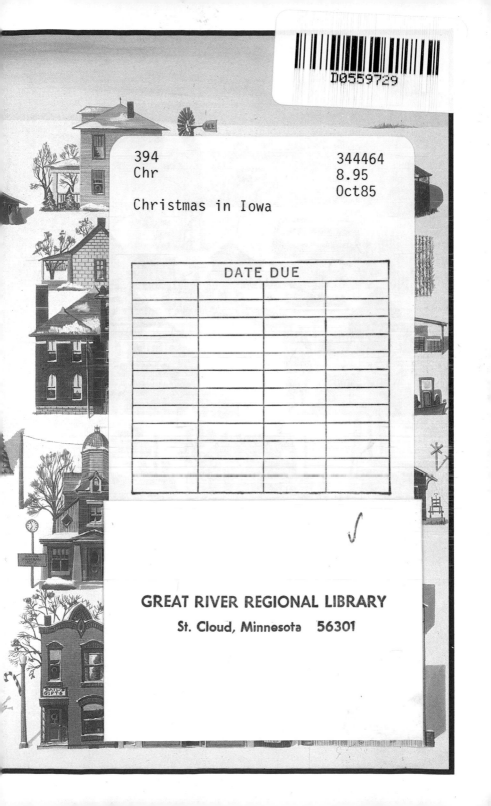

Clarence Andrews

Christmas in
the Midwest

*Clarence Andrews*

# Christmas in Iowa

*By*

Hamlin Garland, Susan Glaspell, Phil Stong, Ruth Suckow, Elizabeth Koren, Hartzell Spence, John Garwood, Bess Streeter Aldrich, James Hearst, Louis Haselmayer, Hadley Read, Katherine Buxbaum, Eva Marie Noé, Marjorie Holmes, Julie McDonald, May Traller, Mildred Freburg Berry, Dorothy Pownall, Robert Dana and Gordon Gammack    *Illustrations by: Stan Haring, John Page, Dean Norman, Felix Summers, Esther Fenske, Lee Burton, Ted Daniels, Lenore Evans and John P. Deniston*

## Midwest Heritage Publishing Company

Iowa City, Iowa

927244

**Clarence A. Andrews** is the author of *A Literary History of Iowa* (1972), *Chicago in Story, A Literary History* (1983), and author/editor of *Growing Up in Iowa* (1978), *Christmas in Iowa* (1979), *Growing Up in the Middle West* (1981) and *This Is Iowa/ A Cavalcade of the Tall Corn State* (1982). He has also compiled a radio script of *The American Dream in the Heartland* (1982).

# ACKNOWLEDGMENTS

"Amana Christmas" from *The Iowan* by permission of Eva Noe.

"Icicles," "Christmas Weather" and "Christmas Tree" from *The Iowan* by permission of Ferner Nuhn.

"The Midwest's First Christmas" from *The Marshalltown Times-Republican*, with an appreciation to John Garwood.

"Christmas in a New Land" from *The Diary of Elisabeth Koren* by permission of the Norwegian-American Historical Association.

"Suzanne's Own Night" and "Journey Into Christmas" from *Journey Into Christmas*, © 1949 by Appleton-Century-Crofts used with permission of Hawthorne Books, Inc.

"Memories of a Swedish Christmas" from *Palimpsest*, by permission of the Iowa State Historical Department/ Division of the State Historical Society.

"The Christmas Season" and "Garden Center Christmas Program" from *Morning Chores and Time Remembered*, by Hadley Read, published by the University of Illinois Press, © by the Board of Trustees of the University of Illinois.

"Cherished and Shared of Old," © 1940 by Susan Glaspell, reprinted by permission of Curtis Brown, Ltd.

"Over the Hills to Grandma's House" and "Grandma's House Held Christmas in its Heart," reprinted by permission of the Des Moines Register and Tribune Company.

"Christmas in the Parsonage" from *Get Thee Behind Me*, used by permission of Hartzell Spence.

Drawing by Felix Summers used by permission of Otha D. Wearin.

"Winter is my Memory Season," from *Today's Health* Magazine December 1967 (©). All rights reserved.

"My Middle West" by F. Scott Fitzgerald, excerpted from *The Great Gatsby.* © 1925 Charles Scribner's Sons; © renewed. Reprinted with the permission of Charles Scribner's Sons.

"The Cut-Glass Christmas" by Susan Allen Toth (*Redbook*, December, 1980) used by permission of the author.

First edition, September, 1984

ISBN 0-934582-06-8

**Table of Contents**

* * * Clarence A. Andrews

# Christmas in the Midwest

 N THIS Christmas smorgasbord, with a garnish by midwest artists and photographers, two dozen midwest writers, natives or residents of this great American Heartland, tell us what Christmas has meant to them from pioneer days to the present. Some turn to fantasies, some to romance, some to nostalgia, some to gentle humor, and some to realistic accounts. The net effet is like those "towers of Christmas treats" that some Christmas gift packagers offer us every year.

Christmas was not, of course native to the middle west — the Indians had nothing like it in their traditions or lore. For all of John Garwood's fancies in "Iowa's First Christmas," the customs and traditions of Christmas came with the white immigrants.

The first Christmas observance in the midwest (it was also one of the earliest on the North American continent) came with the French priests and *voyageur* fur hunters as early as the mid-seventeenth century. Side by side with the "Christ masses" these people observed came the secular revels of the hunters, boatmen and trappers. There were gala Christmas parties in which the Chippewa or Ojibwe Indians joined. The French men danced with the Indian girls, and everyone feasted on sugar cakes, puddings and brandy.

From these parties, it seems, the Indians began to celebrate both Christmas and New Year's Day as "Kissing Days." The Indians would come around to the French camps, male and female, old and young, to give and receive kisses and, perhaps, a piece of cake as well.

By the beginning of the nineteenth century when the English and

Americans had largely replaced the French, Christmas had become a special day in a new sense. On December 25, 1805, Zebulon Pike (who later gave Pike's Peak its name) and his company camped near what later became Brainerd, Minnesota. Pike "gave out two pounds extra of meat, two pounds extra of flour, one gill of whiskey and some tobacco to each man to distinguish the Christmas Day."

A few years later when immigrants from the New England states began to arrive in the midwest, intending to transplant their notions about proper behavior to this even newer New England, they were appalled at the traces of "Kissing Day" which still remained among the Indians, and they were equally disgusted by the hearty Yuletide celebrations they found in regions where there were still strong French influences.

Although these self-exiled former New Englanders no longer felt as their Puritan ancestors once had that such observances of Christmas, or for that matter, any observance of Christmas, were a punishable crime, they did consider the celebrations they witnessed to be pagan, no different from some of the Indian rituals they saw. These newcomers' influence was considerable. One settler commented that Christmas was "not half as much a holiday as Thanksgiving." Indeed, for the school children, classes met as usual.

But the ex-New Englander's hopes of forever suppressing holiday cheer in the new territories was doomed. The newer immigrants from Europe brought with them their ways of celebrating Christmas. Germans brought the fir tree, Kris Kringle, and holiday tables laden with cakes, cookies and pies. Swedes brought the traditional lutefisk and rice porridge dinner, whitewashed their cabin walls, and spread grain for the birds on the tops of houses and barns — a custom they had learned in America from Norwegians.

The Norwegians also imported the customs of announcing one's arrival on a Christmas visit by firing a rifle in the air, brewing up a vat of special holiday beer, and hiding a gift for a girl in a small truss of hay that was pitched through the doorway of her house.

Scandinavians also followed the old country tradition of celebrating two Christmases — the yule feast on December 24th and the Christian holy day meal on the 25th. Yule, the ancient holiday celebrating the sun's "return" to longer days, was observed with parties and presents; Christmas day was spent in church.

Religious services were also important to non-Scandianivan

Lutherans and to Catholics and Episcopalians. But other faiths—particularly the New England Congregationalists—considered the day primarily for children, and the only religious observances were held in Sunday School.

The Dutch brought the character of *Singerclaes* or *Sinterklaas* (a shortening of Sint Nicolaes, the patron saint of children). On Christmas Eve this Saint visited the homes of children, leaving money or presents in the wooden shoes of good children and a bundle of switches in the shoes of bad children. Their Christmas feast featured the *Oly-koek* or doughnut.

Those who settled on the farthest frontiers observed Christmas in their log cabins and sod huts, but because they were often far from market towns, they were forced to "make do." Such a home Christmas was observed at Christmas of 1842 in the settlement of "New York," Iowa, a town which later became Clinton. Eighty-two years later, in 1924, Mrs. Mary Miller recalled how, as a girl of five, she and other members of her family "all hung up our stockings on Christmas eve in our log house. Next morning we were gleeful at finding in each stocking a nice, fat, brown doughnut and some pieces of gaily colored calico." Later Mary's sister made her a doll from the cloth.

While Mary and the other children played outside in the snow, her mother cooked a Christmas dinner of "a great wild turkey her father had shot in the woods" and mincemeat pies. A passing Indian stole one of the pies before it had been baked. Later he returned the empty pie tin complaining that the pie was "no good."

Meanwhile, the men might have gone hunting, or else held a shooting contest in which the winner would have won a turkey.

After the Christmas feast of turkey, roast venison and pork, potatoes, nuts and maple sugar, and [well-baked] pie, the family sat in front of the fireplace "and listened to stories of other Christmas days, way off in Indiana from which Mary Miller's father and mother had come in an ox-cart." Like other midwesterners of the time, the family had made its way west in intervals.

You will find Mary Miller's complete story only in 1924 Iowa newspapers. But in the following pages you'll find several heart-warming tales of pioneer midwest Christmases. (Else) Elisabeth Koren, whose Norwegian-born husband served the beautiful Washington Prairie church in Winneshiek County, Iowa from 1873 until his death in 1910, tells what it was like to observe Christmas in 1853, in the new land, far from her homeland, her friends, and loved ones, a Christmas with only the *promise* of a new life and new friends. Bess Streeter Aldrich, whose mother drove an ox-drawn covered wagon from Indiana to eastern Iowa, reconstructs an 1855 Christmas from tales her mother told her—Mrs. Streeter is the "Suzanne" of the story. Hamlin Garland nostalgically recalls an 1860s boyhood Christmas in the Wisconsin coulee country and an 1870s Christmas on the prairies of northeast Iowa.

Throughout the nineteenth century, midwest Christmases became a blend of traditions and customs. By the time of the Civil War, in part owing to such literary classics as Clement Moore's "The Night Before Christmas" (1823) and Charles Dickens's *Christmas Carol* (1843), the Puritan influence was declining. In St. Paul, Charles Emerson, editor of the St. Paul *Daily Democrat,* helped spread the idea of a "merry" Christmas by urging St. Paul residents to indulge in the holiday spirit. Each Christmas his paper carried glowing accounts of Christmas activities in the Twin Cities:

> *Skating on the Mississippi near the lower landing was very extensive on Christmas day. A goodly number of ladies honored the day with their presence. The carnival was at its height about 4 p.m. when it seemed that all St. Paul had determined to do a little skating. There was good skating and poor skating, skating with the skates on the ice, and skating with the skates in the air!*

In addition to such secular activities, there were also celebrations of the birth of the Babe in the manger. Some of these celebrations are described here in the story of a Moravian Christmas with its Festival of Lights and no Santa Claus; of a Swedish Christmas somewhat modified because the Swedish family dwelt in a German neighborhood; of an Amana Christmas which originally focused on a German "pyramid" of wood, later on the "Tannenbaum" and a visit from "Sankt Nikolaus"; of a Danish Christmas with its legend that the animals talked at midnight on Christmas Eve.

The Christmas tree was not a part of early midwest observances, but came after Christmas of 1841, following the gift of a Christmas tree to the English Queen Victoria from her German-born Prince Consort. At first, as Hamlin Garland tells us in his "My First Christmas Tree," the pioneers' trees were set up in their churches.

In the early days settlers would look in nearby groves for an evergreen or other small tree which would serve as a Christmas tree. But as more settlers arrived it became necessary to import trees from the north woods of Minnesota, Wisconsin and Michigan, and to bring them by ship to lake cities and river cities for distribution. You will find later on the heartwarming story of the "Chicago Christmas Tree Ship," a major Windy City institution for over half a century.

In time there came to be more of an emphasis on commercial gifts, rather than hand-made ones. In 1872, a midwest visitor from Stockholm, Sweden related his reaction to this change:

> *Much activity prevailed in St. Paul when I got there. The handsome stores were filled with newly arrived articles which were tasteful and often rather costly, intended as gifts for the coming holidays. There was a brisk sale of Christmas trees in the markets and those streets along which the retailers had their shops were crowded with conveyances belonging to nearby farmers who were in town to buy gifts or delicacies for the Christmas table. . . . So far as the number and costliness of the presents are concerned, the shoppers often display a liberality that would amaze us Swedish natives.*

A Merry Midwest Christmas to you!

*Clarence and Ollie Andrews*

*December Afternoon*
Grant Wood, 1941

* * * John Garwood

# Iowa's First Christmas

T WAS a clear, cold, starlight night. A blanket of the whitest snow bedded down the valley of the Iowa. There were no lights from farms or villages because there were no farms or villages. It was almost two thousand years ago!

Like the blanket of snow which covered the valley a blanket of peace mantled the heavens, and each twinkling star seemed to send down a message to the wildlife of the valley. It was a special night and, from the snow owl in the highest tree to the muskrat splashing in an open riffle of the river, all seemed aware of a difference.

A rabbit hopped from beneath a shelter of hazel brush. Sitting on his haunches he nibbled bits of sky with his nose. He knew that a fox was stalking his tracks but on this "special" night he had no fear—only peaceful security. Slowly he made his way to the top of a treeless hill...attracted by what, he did not know. The fox followed.

Pausing at the crest of the hill the rabbit sat up and turned his head toward the east where a bright and shining star shed its brilliant glow over the countryside. Behind came the fox intent on the kill. Then, too, he saw the star—and sitting down beside the rabbit he raised his head toward the skies.

From the shadowy woods, from the river and from the open prairie came the wildlife of the valley of the Iowa. A doe and a fawn, a lumbering bear, two skulking wolves and a white weasel all took places in a great semi-circle beside the fox and the rabbit. All, unaware of each other, gazed at the great star in the east. From the river came the mink, the muskrat, the beaver and the otter. From the woods came the raccoon, the opossum, and the badger. A lynx and a skunk wandered the same path leading to the hill, where they joined with the others in their vigil of the star. Then came a shaggy buffalo to join the silent group.

The brilliance of the star in the east wakened the birds of the valley and they too were attracted to the hill. There, the prairie chicken, the wild turkey and the quail roosted with the hawk and the owl. Far below in the valley three old geese, the wisest of birds, placidly rode the open ripples of the river.

Swiftly and silently, along a game trail near the river, came a hunter in search of food and fur for his wigwam. A flint axe hung from his belt. Seeing the many tracks leading from the river he followed them upward to the hill. The light of the star cast a brilliance on the wildlife assembled there. Swiftly he bent an arrow to his bow and took aim at the doe, the nearest. Then he too saw the star in the east and slowly lowered his arms. Gazing in wonder he strode silently forward and took a place beside the buffalo.

From the river came the sound of the beating of strong wings as the three old geese took off from the water. Circling slowly above the assembled birds, beasts and hunter they set a course straight toward the star in the east.

The hunter watched them until they could be seen no more. Then, turning, he gazed at the wildlife about him. Slowly he returned his arrows to their quiver, unstrung the bow, and silently strode away into the night.

There was peace in the valley of the Iowa.

—*Marshalltown Times-Republican* 1956

* * * Elisabeth Koren

# Christmas in a New Land

*HRISTMAS EVE, 1853:* This was a strange Christmas Eve, indeed; so different from any I have ever known before. Here we sat, Vilhelm and I, separated for the first time from relatives and friends, in a little log cabin far inland in America. For supper we had spareribs and coffee. As we sit here now, we get a little light from a lead dish in which there are tallow scraps and a little rag for a wick, placed on an overturned salt container. Vilhelm is studying his sermon for tomorrow. We are expecting Erik [Egge, our host] back from Decorah any moment; he is bringing the bed in which are we to sleep, as well as some candles.

After dinner today, Nils [Hanson Katterud] hitched up his oxen. We said farewell to our friendly hosts [the Katterud family], promised to visit them often, and seated ourselves in the sleigh, Vilhelm on the chest in back, I on the chest in front, holding on as best we could, for the road was not what you would call smooth. . . . At last, right side up, we halted the oxen outside [the Egges'] house, and entered a room which, though clean, did not have the most pleasing odor, because it had just been scrubbed by Helene, mistress of the house.

. . . Helene, who appears to be a kind, friendly woman, brought out beer and *fattigmandsbakkels* ["poor man's cake," a favorite Norwegian pastry]; after that, accompanied by Per and Kari, three and four years old, we went up to the loft to put our things somewhat in order. I cannot imagine how Vilhelm will get any quiet for study here, it will be so crowded.

What a contrast between this evening and a year ago! I am happy and content that we are here in time for the Christmas festival—there is such joy over the pastor's coming—but it grieves me to think of Father and the others whom I miss, for the first time, on this Christmas Eve.

Vilhelm took a walk with me. The evening is lovely; it was good to get outside a little. Oh, how beautiful the sky is! The stars are much brighter and seem larger than at home. . . .

*First Christmas Day Evening.* Today, before a large group of listeners, Vilhelm preached his first sermon. The service was held in the largest room they could find, at the home of Thorgrim Busness. When the service was over, I talked with several people—as many as I could, for it was so crowded that one could not move. It pleases and interests me to see and talk to all these different people, our Norwegian farm folk, with whom I have had so little acquaintance up to this time.

I find many of them attractive; I like those best who have no city flourish about them, but come up, take me by the hand and say, "Well, we wish you welcome to America!" Then, generally, a number of questions follow. "Where do you come from? Have you parents and relatives? There was great sorrow when you were to leave, I imagine?" Also at times, "My, that is a lovely brooch you have there!" followed by careful examination and admiration of what I am wearing. . . .

*Second Christmas Day.* We came back a little while ago from Ingebret Haugen's. I am very glad I went; otherwise I should have missed an enjoyable day. At eight-thirty Nils stopped outside the door with his two daughters, who were to go with us. There was a cold wind. Helene had lent me a good heavy coat, so I was warm enough to enjoy the beautiful drive.

The road went up and down hill, through a long, narrow, unusual valley, where there were rocks like those near the high ridges along the Wisconsin River. When we passed through the valley, we saw the Little Iowa River, along the banks of which, as everywhere along the rivers here, it is very beautiful, though only sparsely settled.

Not far from there lies Decorah, which looks at least more imposing than Milton and has a pretty location. A couple of miles beyond is Ingebret's house, where the service was to be held that day; it is on the edge of a large wood where there is said to be an abundance of wild grapes and other fruits.

We came into a good-sized room with two beds, one above the

other, along the wall; in the lower of these lay the husband, who had been sickly for a long time. The remaining furniture of the room consisted of a large motley-painted cupboard and a second one of black walnut, a wood which is beautiful for furniture (though the farmers much prefer fir painted in gaudy colors), a table, chairs, the usual stove—in the center of one wall—and a hole in the ceiling, through which a stairway leads up to the loft; the rest of the room was filled with rough planks laid upon blocks cut from trees, upon which some members of the congregation had already taken seats.

Erik Egge Home—Decorah
Luther College Library

The lady of the house, Ingrid, a neat, active farm woman who still wears part of her national costume, helped me off with my wraps, got me a seat, offered me something to drink, and showed her friendliness in many ways. . . .

I enjoyed being there and talking with people; there were many openhearted, fine folk. A young, handsome woman from Valdres (Ola

Bergan was her husband's name, I think) won my heart especially. I also met both the sisters of Pastor Brandt and their husbands, friendly people who have retained their Valdres dialect; they pressed us to visit them when services are to be held in their neighborhood. I also enjoyed talking with an old woman from Valdres who knew Christie when he was pastor there and who was very eager to get news of all the children. . . .

It was a pleasant drive home, for it was no longer blowing. Anne and Knud entertained us with horrid stories of snakes, and we made fast progress until we came to Thrond Lommen's. There we simply had to turn in, for he is Knud's best friend, he said, and it would not do to pass him by.

The entrance to Thrond's house is not very nice; one has to cross an area something like a dunghill, where horses, oxen, cattle, swine, hens, and all kinds of four-legged and two-legged creatures wander about amiably together. Thrond lives in a very large room which houses, besides him and his family, also half a score of newcomers for the winter. His elderly wife met me with many heartfelt and pious wishes that our coming hither might be a blessing for us and others.

After we had tasted her Christmas beer, we hurried away to reach home before darkness fell; but it overtook us just the same. . . .

—from *The Diary of Elisabeth Koren* (translated from the original Norwegian by David T. Nelson), 1955.

* * * Hamlin Garland

# A Pioneer Christmas

HE FIRST Christmas that I seem to remember fully has a wonderful quality to me. Like a picture by Rembrandt it has but one side defined, the other melts away into shadow—luminous shadow, where faint light pulses across and lures the wistful gaze on and on into the unfathomable, where beginnings lie hidden.

The first I recall of my first Christmas I am riding behind my parents in a huge sleigh, amid high snowdrifts, sculptured into strange forms by the prairie winds. It is growing dusk. Before us in a similar sleigh my young uncle, a giant in size, leads the way. I can see him outlined against the dull orange sky. He stands erect, holding the reins of his swiftly-moving horses in one of his powerful hands; occasionally he shouts back to my father, who is buried in a thick buffalo-hide coat. My mother is only another figure wrapped in shawls.

My sister and brother are beside me under the blankets on the straw. My brother is asleep, but I am on my knees looking ahead. I see now my uncle silhouetted on the dull orange notch between two deep purple banks of trees. That is the place where the road pierces the woods. Suddenly, with rush of wind and jingle of bells, we enter the darkness of the forest, and the road begins to climb.

I cannot remember much after that: I suppose I grew sleepy. I have a dim memory of climbing hills, of the squall of sleigh-runners over bridges, and of the gurgle of ice-bound water, but it is all fused with dreams.

I was roused at last by the vigorous touch of my uncle and his hearty voice: "Wake up an' pay y'r lodgin'." I looked up and saw father standing beside the sleigh. I saw the dark branches of trees overhead, and heard the sound of many voices from the warmly-lighted little cabin's open door.

I bundled out, heavy with cold and sleep. As I stood there my uncle reached up his arms to take my mother down, not knowing of the rheumatism in her wrists. She gave a sharp scream, and my uncle's team started away on a swift run round the curve of the road toward the gate.

I stood like one in a dream, seeing the flying team and the wonderful race of my uncle toward the gate to intercept the runaways. He ran silently, with magnificent action, his head thrown up. As the team dashed through the gate his left hand caught the end board, and then I saw nothing further of the runaway.

We went into the house. It was a little house with two main rooms, the kitchen and the sitting-room. In the sitting-room was an open fireplace, the first I had ever seen—a wonder and a delight.

The women folks talked and laughed, creating an atmosphere of good cheer. We children were put to warm before the fire, where grandfather sat, a reticent and smiling old man of great size.

I suppose the room was poor enough, but I did not see that in the glow of that open fireplace. I heard my young and pretty Aunt Rebecca out in the kitchen opening oyster-cans—a great treat were oysters to us—and Aunt Deborah brought us in a handful of wonderful little crackers.

Mother sat out in the kitchen near the table and visited with my aunts while they worked. Soon father came "stomping" in with his hearty voice dominating the laughter of the women.

"Got anything good to eat?"

"Not unless you brought it," replied my saucy Aunt Deborah.

"Well, I guess I'll go home again. What's the use o' goin' visitin' unless you git somethin' better'n common?"

The women asked about the runaway but father knew as little as they about it. At last my Uncle David came in.

"Did you stop 'em?" everybody asked.

"You bet," he replied in his laconic way. "How's them oysters? I'm holler as a beech log."

The fragrance of the oyster soup wakened me more than the loud, hearty talk, and when we drew round the table in the little lean-to kitchen every face shone with the light of Christmas. The big pan of oyster soup (which we had only two or three times a year) and the paper bag of crackers formed the entire meal. It was an oyster supper in full of the term.

Slowly, one by one, the company drew back, and a subdued jollity succeeded as all went back to the sitting-room. There among the women, a few patterns were shown and exchanged, while the men told stories of logging and hunting, and bears and wolves and Indians.

The children listened with scared and fascinated souls, till at last father (who couldn't whistle a tune, but who never got enough of music) called out in his peremptory way:

"Come on, get that fiddle out, Dave. Deb, open up that melodeon."

Ah! that was the best part of it all—the music. It made Christmas worth while. It was sweeter than oyster soup.

Uncle David played—old dance tunes that have passed from fiddler to fiddler until they have become veritable folk-songs. Then they all sang while he twanged the fiddle like a guitar, as an accompaniment. Aunt Deborah and mother sang "Nellie Wildwood," and "Belle Malone," and "The Drummer Boy," and then father demanded all the old war songs—"Just Before the Battle, Mother," and "The Battle Cry of Freedom," and "The Day of Jubilee."

Tired of singing at last, Uncle David struck into "Honest John" or some other old-fashioned square dance. One of my aunts came skipping across the room to where my father sat. There was saucy daring in her attitudes.

"Come on, old man!" she said. The war had made my father bent and stiff before his time, but he sprang up.

"I don't take no such stump as that!" he shouted. The rest laughed, and Uncle Frank drew a broom-stick along the floor making hideous howls. Uncle David played on absorbedly, while we children shrieked with delight to see father bow and scrape and dance all sorts of double-shuffles and single-shuffles and break-downs. Mother joined in too, and it seemed very wonderful to us. Grandfather smiled and patted his knees in time to the music.

"Oh, I'm too old!" shouted father as he dropped back into a chair, and the gale of fun ended as quickly as it had begun. Laughing and breathing hard, they all took seats and fell into silence, facing the fire, and Uncle David, his soul mellowed and subdued, played wild, strange tunes he had picked up somewhere without instruction—almost without repetition—strangely sweet and weird to me, worth infinitely more than Christmas presents.

Love songs some of them were, full of sombre, longing inflections, which I could dimly feel, but could not understand.

He played "Maggie, Air You Sleepin'?" and the wind outside went to my soul. Voices cried to me out of the cold and illimitable hill-land forests—voices that pleaded and wept:

> *"Oh, let me in, for loud the linn*
> *Goes roarin' o'er the moorland craggy."*

My uncle's handsome face grew sad, somehow, in the midst of happiness. He forgot his young wife and his sisters; his eyes looked away into storms, the future seemed to menace him.

He stopped abruptly, and put the violin away in its box as if to hide his emotion.

My father broke the silence with an abrupt sigh.

"Well, well! Look here, 's time you youngsters climbed the stairs. Becky, where do these fellers go?"

Aunt Rebecca looked at us reflectively. "Well, now, I don't know. I guess we'll need to make a bed here on the floor."

"Goody!" cried my brother, "then we'll see Santa Claus!"

The older people looked at each other amd smiled. With the indifferent air of one who has a perfect understanding of it all, I scorned to be so silly.

"Mighty little you'll see of Santa Claus this night," said my aunt. "He can't get down here on such a night as this."

For once in my life I was to be able to hang my stocking before a fireplace, and it revived my waning enthusiasm. Mother, with her abounding drollery, hung up the big stocking which went over her shoes. Everybody laughed at everybody's joke, and soon everything was arranged for the night.

I felt the illimitable presence of the forests to the north. To my child-mind this cabin was like a ship set in gray seas would seem to me now. All I knew of the world was in the tales my father told. The road we had come ran back a slender and desolate track, back to the Wisconsin *coulée* we had left behind—I could not tell the direction of it. Then my mind came back in a strange way to a visit I had made somewhere to a dark, swift stream which ran under a little bridge. There was a mysterious bag moored there by a rope, and it suggested bags of gold and robbers someway. It swung to and fro with a wild motion. It grew dusk as I looked, and the wind grew cold and I ran away as fast as possible and—my eyes came open and I realized I had been dreaming in the first stages of sleep.

I could hear the women laughing and moving about, and I lost my shiver of fear very soon. I heard the rattle of paper bags and parcels. I knew it was my duty to go to sleep, but I couldn't compose myself to do it. People slept close together in those days. Making a bed on the floor was too common to call for comment. The men gave up the beds to the women and went noisily upstairs to camp down on the floor of the low chamber. There was no fear of ventilation up-stairs or down. The wind drove the cold under the door, and along the floor the frost crept.

I lay facing the fireplace, after all had become still, hearing the trees soughing outside, hearing the sad wail of a cat at the barn and watching the fire die away—but when the deep sleep of childhood came upon me I forgot Santa Claus and the stocking. I woke in the early light to hear Uncle David building the fire, and then came my brother's outcries and the hurly-burly of good cheer and hearty greeting from old and young. Mother's big stocking was overflowing with potatoes and wads of paper, with some little present far down at the toe. Everybody had something, if it were nothing more than an old door-knob or a doughnut.

We children had tin horses and tin soldiers, and monkeys on sticks (poor pathetic little toys these), and best of all, candy—wonderful candies of all conceivable sorts! The war had made candies an almost unattainable luxury—but Christmas would be empty and a hollow mockery without candy and nuts ("boughten nuts," not hazel nuts and hickory nuts, of which we had plenty, but the other strange kinds).

The hurly-burly lasted until breakfast was called, and everybody who could find places sat around and attacked the venison and potatoes which formed the meal.

The forenoon passed quickly with sleigh-rides with Uncle David, with games with the tin horses, and the dinner came, for which the youngsters had little appetite. Turkey bowed humbly before candy. I do not seem to remember leave-taking, or the ride homeward. I remember only the desolate cold of the kitchen at home, into which we tramped and sat in our wraps until the fire began to roar in its iron cage.

Oh, winds of the winter night! Oh, fire-light and the shine of tender eyes! How far away you seem tonight, so faint and far, each dear face shineth as a star.

Oh, uncle by the Western sea beyond the reach of Christmas snow, does not your heart hunger like mine tonight, for that Christmas eve among the trees—for the shine of undimmed eyes, for the hair untouched by gray, for the quaint, great figure seated in sombre reverie beside the fire?

It all lies in the unchanging land of the past. Its charm, its strange dominion cannot be felt again, except in reminiscent dream. No money, no railway train can take us back to it. Its power was the mystical union of youth, fire-light, great forests, music and the voice of moaning winds. A union which can never come again to you or me, father, mother, brother, any more than the Iowa prairies can return again, unscarred by spade and plough.

—*The Ladies Home Journal* December, 1893

* * * Bess Streeter Aldrich

# Suzanne's Own Night

HRISTMAS EVE of 1855 in the Martins' big log-and-frame house there at the edge of the grove which swept up from the timberland along Iowa's Red Cedar River!

It was very cold. Several settlers had frozen to death in near-by localities, so said the papers. There was a little newspaper in each town now, the *Iowa State Register* in Prairie Rapids, the *Banner* in Sturgis Falls. That was progress for you.

The west windows in the lean-to were packed solid with snow, the east ones only less so by a few square inches of peep holes. The main room was warm as far as the fire from the four-foot logs could throw its heat. Beyond that it was as cold as though one stepped into another climate. In Sarah's bedroom the frost sparkled on the whitewashed logs of the walls. Up the loft ladders the east bedroom was only less cold than the outdoors by the slight advantage given from a roof breaking the sweep of prairie wind. The west loft had one mildly warm spot in it. By standing with your back flattened against the wall where the fireplace chimney passed through, you could detect a faint response of heat.

But as standing with your back flattened to a chimney was inconvenient for any protracted period, the inmates of the west chamber were as near to a state of freezing as those of the east. All the girls wore flannel nightgowns, flannel nightcaps, and flannel bed-socks, and rather perilously, with much squealing, carried up the ladders each night pieces of hot soapstone wrapped in fragments of clean worn rugs. Safely up the ladders without having dropped hot stones on whoever came behind, they climbed onto feather-beds, pulled other feather-stuffed ticks and several pieced comforts over them, and if their clattering tongues ceased and their exuberant spirits calmed down sufficiently soon, were not long in going soundly to sleep.

To-night all were around the fireplace except Sabina, who was over in her Sturgis Falls home getting ready her first Christmas dinner for them all on the morrow. Henry and Lucy had come over from the other house so there were still eleven people. Lucy sat in Ma's red-covered rocker out of deference to her delicate condition, a concession that had its humorous side when one stopped to think that all year she had washed, ironed, baked, scrubbed, made soap, hoed in the garden, gone after the cows in the timber, and on occasion helped milk. But this was Christmas Eve and all at once every one was deferential to the Madonna-like potentialities of Lucy.

Christmas Eve was Suzanne's own night. It had been made for her. Sitting on the floor with her back to the edge of the fireplace, arms around her knees while the light played over the room, she had that feeling which always came with this special night. She could not put it into words which satisfied her, but in some vague way knew it was magic—the night for which one lived all year.

In the summer, with the mourning-doves and the bouncing-Bets, the wild grape-vine swings and the long walks in the timber, you forgot entirely the feeling that this night could bring. To think of it gave you no emotion whatever. In the early fall you began to remember it. By November it became a bright light toward which you walked. And now to-night you could not think with one bit of excitement how much you liked the summer things. Yes, it was magic. The snow piled against the window was not like other snows. The wind in the chimney was not like other winds. If you scratched a frosted place out of which to look, you saw that the snowpacked prairie to the north was a white country in which no other person lived, that the snowpacked timberland to the south was a white woods forever silent. It was as though there were no human at all in any direction but your own family. Christmas Eve was a white light that drew a magic circle around the members of your own family to hem them all in and fasten them together.

Every one was laughing and talking there in front of the fire where the long knitted stockings hung. Soon now they would all get up and go after the funny-shaped packages hidden in drawers and under beds and put them in the stockings. Suzanne had something for every one—a little pincushion fitted into a river shell for each girl, a fancy box for Ma, with tiny shells fastened thick on it with glue made from old Rosy's hoofs, handkerchiefs hemmed from an outgrown petticoat for Pa, Phineas, and Henry, a corn-cob doll for—she still felt undecided whether or not it would be quite nice to put a corn-cob doll in Lucy's stocking.

The pale yellow light from the tallow candles on the shelf and the brighter reddish light from the wood logs made all the faces stand out from the darkness behind them.

Something about the magic of this night made the folks seem queer and different, too. You could not tell why, but to-night every poor quality about them fell away and only the good ones remained—Pa's big certainty that his way was always right, Ma's scolding, Henry's stubborn quietness, Phineas' smart-Aleck ways, Emily's freckled homeliness, Jeanie's silly changeableness, Phoebe Lou's teasing, Melinda's rough tomboyishness, Celia's vanity. Her heart warmed to them all.

"I'll never think of those imaginary people again," she told herself. "I'll just stay by my own real folks."

Pa was telling about Christmastime back in England; things his grandfather had told him that had come down in the tales from there—about the piping and dancing, the carols and the maskers and the woodcocks cooked in gin. "My great-grandfather's family was landed gentry back in the mother country. Ma's ancestor hung the light in Old North Church when the British was comin'. Ma says her father told her the man was to hang one light if they come by land and two if they was comin' by sea. Both sides they bore arms for the country, faithful and loyal. You children don't never need to take a back seat for anybody. Just hold up your head and speak up all your lives. Both sides good landed-gentry blood runs in your veins and..."

If you listened above the din of the talking you could hear the wind in the chimney turn into music. Christmas Eve was a night of song that wrapped itself about you like a shawl. But it warmed more than your body. It warmed your heart...filled it, too, with melody that would last forever. Even though you grew up and found you could

never quite bring back the magic feeling of this night, the melody
would stay in your heart always—a song for all the years.

—*Song of Years* 1939

\* \* \* Hamlin Garland

# My First Christmas Tree

E NEVER had a Christmas tree in our house in the Wisconsin coulée; indeed, my father never saw one in a family circle till he saw that which I set up for my own children last year. But we celebrated Christmas in those days, always, and I cannot remember a time when we did not all hang up our stockings for "Sandy Claws" to fill. As I look back upon those days it seems as if the snows were always deep, the night skies crystal clear, and the stars especially lustrous with frosty sparkles of blue and yellow fire—and probably this was so, for we lived in a Northern land where winter was usually stern and always long.

I recall one Christmas when "Sandy" brought me a sled, and a horse that stood on rollers—a wonderful tin horse which I very shortly split in two in order to see what his insides were. Father traded a cord of wood for the sled and the horse cost twenty cents—but they made the day wonderful.

Another notable Christmas Day, as I stood in our front yard, mid-leg deep in snow, a neighbor drove by closely muffled in furs, while behind his seat his son, a lad of twelve or fifteen, stood beside a barrel of apples, and as he passed he hurled a glorious big red one at me. It missed me, but bored a deep, round hole in the soft snow. I thrill yet with the remembered joy of of burrowing for that delicious bomb. Nothing will ever smell as good as that Wine Sap or Northern Spy or whatever it was. It was a wayward impulse on the part of the boy in the sleigh, but it warms my heart after more than forty years.

We had no chimney in our home, but the stocking-hanging was a ceremony, nevertheless. My parents, and especially my mother, entered into it with the best of humor. They always put up their own stockings or permitted us to do it for them—and they always laughed next morning when they found potatoes or ears of corn in them. I can see now that my mother's laugh had a tear in it, for she loved pretty things and seldom got any during the years that we lived in the coulée.

When I was ten years old [in 1870] we moved to Mitchell County, an Iowa prairie land, and there we prospered in such wise that our stockings always held toys of some sort, and even my mother's stocking occasionally sagged with a simple piece of jewelry or a new comb or brush. But the thought of a family Christmas tree remained the luxury of millionaire city dwellers; indeed it was not till my fifteenth or sixteenth year that our Sunday school rose to the extravagance of a tree, and it is of this wondrous festival that I write.

The land about us was only partially cultivated at this time, and our district school house, a bare little box, was set bleakly on the prairie; but the Burr Oak school house was not only larger but it stood beneath great oaks as well and possessed the charm of a forest background through which a stream ran silently. It was our chief social center. There of a Sunday night a regular preacher held "Divine service" with Sunday school as a sequence. At night—usually on Friday nights—the young people let in "lyceums," as we called them, to debate great questions or to "speak pieces" and read essays; and here it was that I saw my first Christmas tree.

I walked to that tree across four miles of moonlit snow. Snow? No, it was a floor of diamonds, a magical world, so beautiful that my heart still aches with the wonder of it and with the regret that it has all gone—gone with the keen eyes and the bounding pulses of the boy.

Our home at this time was a small frame house on the prairie almost directly west of the Burr Oak grove, and as it was too cold to take the horses out, my brother and I, with our tall boots, our visored caps and long woolen mufflers, started forth afoot defiant of the cold. We left the gate on the trot, bound for a sight of the glittering unknown. The snow was deep and we moved side by side in the grooves made by the hoofs of the horses, setting our feet in the shine left by the broad shoes of the wood sleighs whose going had smoothed the way for us.

Our breaths rose like smoke in the still air. It must have been ten below zero, but that did not trouble us in those days, and at last we came in sight of the lights, in the sound of the singing, the laughter, the bells of the feast.

It was a poor little building without tower or bell and its low walls had but three windows on a side, and yet it seemed very imposing to me that night as I crossed the threshold and faced the strange people who packed it to the door. I say "strange people," for though I had seen most of them many times they all seemed somehow alien to me that night. I was an irregular attendant at Sunday school and did not expect a present, therefore I stood against the wall and gazed with open-eyed marveling at the shining pine which stood where the pulpit was wont to be. I was made to feel the more embarrassed by reason of the remark of a boy who accused me of having forgotten to comb my hair.

This was not true, but the cap I wore always matted my hair down over my brow, and then, when I lifted it off invariably disarranged it completely. Nevertheless I felt guilty—and hot. I don't suppose my hair was artistically barbered that night—I rather guess Mother had used the shears—and I can believe that I looked the half-wild colt that I was; but there was no call for that youth to direct attention to my unavoidable shagginess.

I don't think the tree had many candles, and I don't remember that it glittered with golden apples. But it was loaded with presents, and the girls coming and going clothed in bright garments made me forget my own looks—I think they made me forget to remove my overcoat, which was a sodden thing of poor cut and worse quality. I think I must have stood agape for nearly two hours listening to the songs, noting every motion of Adironam Burtch and Asa Walker as they directed the ceremonies and prepared the way for the great event—that is to say, for the coming of Santa Claus himself.

A furious jingling of bells, a loud voice outside, the lifting of a window, the nearer clash of bells, and the dear old Saint appeared (in the person of Stephen Bartle) clothed in a red robe, a belt of sleigh bells, and a long white beard. The children cried out, "Oh!" The girls tittered and shrieked with excitement, and the boys laughed and clapped their hands. Then "Sandy" made a little speech about being glad to see us all, but as he had many other places to visit, and as there were a great many presents to distribute, he guessed he'd have to ask some of the many pretty girls to help him. So he called upon Betty

Burtch and Hattie Knapp—and I for one admired his taste, for they were the most popular maids of the school.

They came up blushing, and a little bewildered by the blaze of publicity thus thrown upon them. But their native dignity asserted itself, and the distribution of the presents began. I have a notion now that the fruit upon the tree was mostly bags of popcorn and "corny copias" of candy, but as my brother and I stood there that night and saw everybody, even the rowdiest boy, getting something we felt aggrieved and rebellious. We forgot that we had come from afar—we only knew that we were being left out.

But suddenly, in the midst of our gloom, my brother's name was called, and a lovely girl with a gentle smile handed him a bag of popcorn. My heart glowed with gratitude. Somebody had thought of us; and when she came to me, saying sweetly, "Here's something for you," I had not words to thank her. This happened nearly forty years ago, but her smile, her outstretched hand, her sympathetic eyes are vividly before me as I write. She was sorry for the shockheaded boy who stood against the wall, and her pity made the little box of candy a casket of pearls. The fact that I swallowed the jewels on the road home does not take from the reality of my adoration.

At last I had to take my final glimpse of that wondrous tree, and I well remember the walk home. My brother and I traveled in wordless companionship. The moon was sinking toward the west, and the snow crusted with a million fairy lamps, The sentinel watchdogs barked from lonely farmhouses, and the wolves answered from the ridges. Now and then sleighs passed us with lovers sitting two and two, and the bells on their horses had the remote music of romance to us whose boots drummed like clogs of wood upon the icy road.

Our house was dark as we approached and entered it, but how deliciously warm it seemed after the pitiless wind! I confess we made straight for the cupboard for a mince pie, a doughnut and a bowl of milk!

As I write this [in 1911] there stands in my library a thick-branched, beautifully tapering fir tree covered with the gold and purple apples of Hesperides, together with crystal ice points, green and red and yellow candles, clusters of gilded grapes, wreaths of metallic frost, and glittering angels swinging in ecstasy; but I doubt if my children will ever know the keen pleasure (that is almost pain) which came to my brother and me in those Christmas days when an orange was not a breakfast fruit, but a casket of incense and spice, a message from the sunlands of the South.

That was our compensation—we brought to our Christmastime a keen appetite and empty hands. And the lesson of it all is, if we are seeking a lesson, that it is better to give to those who want than to those for whom "we ought to do something because they did something for us last year."

—*The Ladies Home Journal* December 1911

*Schoolhouse in the Snow*
John Page, 1979

* * * May Traller

# Over the Hills to Grandma's House

 E ALWAYS used to go to Grandma's for Christmas, and memory re-creates on each of those glamorous Christmas eves a snowstorm, beginning with great tentative flakes wandering through the whispering branches, then thickening until the air was a-swirl with a curtain of white.

Dad always hitched up Deck and Puss to the farm wagon, for no car could get through the lane that led from Burney Meadow to the valley where Grandma's farm lay. Dad piled an armload of straw into the wagon bed and covered it with an old comfort dedicated to the purpose.

We children climbed onto the soft seat and mother tucked another old quilt about us. They placed mysterious boxes in the wagon, then climbed to the spring seat.

I can still hear the whisper of steel tires on the newly-fallen snow as we drove through the woods, over the hill and past the bois d'arc hedge windbreak. The bushes would be bending over with the white weight, and the world would present a wide expanse of snow that seemed a very part of Christmas. Puss and Deck, their hoof beats muffled in the flakes, trotted with unwonted briskness along the lane.

At the top of Burney Hill where dad had to set the brake hard, we children always got up on our knees to watch the perilous descent and to catch the first glimpse of Grandma's long, low house set among its cedars and locusts. There it would be at the bottom of the hill, its squat stone chimney smoking like a friendly old pioneer. There Grandma would be on the long front porch, waving to us, and Elza, the hired man, would be coming in with another log for the fireplace.

Inside Grandma's big living room all would be a warm, rosy bloom as the flames danced in fantastic welcome about the huge fireplace.

"Aw-w-w, shucks," Elza would always exclaim. "I meant to get a Christmas tree but I just smack forgot about it. We'll just have to do without this year."

Of course the statement always brought a clamor of protests from us, and Elza pretended penitence. "Aw-w-w, shucks," he would say at last. "We'll go out and see if Santa Claus marked any tree for us. You know we can't chop down any that Santa hasn't marked. It wouldn't be proper."

And we agreed tremblingly, because we were certain that a tree must have been marked for us up in Grandma's south woods.

Grandma made us pull on long woolen stockings over our shoes and up over our knees for wading the drifts, and besides she made us carry a hot boiled potato in our mittened hands for warmth. There is something that warms even your heart when you carry a hot boiled potato in each hand as you climb over rock fences, plunge through knee-deep drifts and creep under a tangle of evergreens and bittersweet while the snow still comes down thickly and silently.

We followed Elza closely as he peered about for a sign left upon a tree by Santa, and our hearts sank when he said, "Aw-w-w, shucks, Santa didn't leave any sign. I guess we'll have to go back."

But when he saw tears behind our doubtful expressions, he cried, "Aw-w-w shucks! There is Santa's mark, right over there!" And sure enough, there would be a fat little cedar tree with a red bandanna tied to it. Santa's mark indeed!

What a triumphant journey we made with that tree down the hill! We lugged it and still held onto our boiled potato, which had kept our hands warm and happy, until we reached the long front porch. There we made a ceremony of leaving the potatoes for the birds and dragged the tree into the rosy lighted living room.

Elza set it up with much ado and many an "Aw-w-w, shucks," and when it was standing there with the firelight glowing upon its shiny branches, life was good indeed.

Supper was a feast, because the trip through the snowy woods had made us ravenous. Grandma always had egg-butter and hot biscuits for the Christmas Eve meal; if you haven't eaten egg-butter, you have missed a great joy.

Afterwards we sat in the firelight gazing at our tree and listening to the Christmas tales Grandma always told, wonder stories which grew more beautiful each year.

And listening to the sound of the envious sleet tapping at the window and to the crackling fire, we would grow drowsy and snuggle closer together. Our gay little tree seemed to be spreading protecting Christmas wings over us as Grandma sang the sweet old song—

*"Star in the east, the horizon adorning,*
*Guide where our Infant Redeemer was laid."*

The next I knew I was being held up so I could poke a stocking at the nail in the fireboard, and someone was carrying me up to the attic room, which was warmed by the huge old chimney. Just above my head there was the tap-tappity-tap of lazy sleet on the roof. Down, down, I sank into the feathered bed, into velvety blackness, into dreamless sleep.

Early next morning we would be awakened by the smell of breakfast cooking, and by Elza's voice in simulated surprise. "Aw-w-w shucks! Santa Claus did get here after all!"

We would tumble out of bed and race down stairs shouting, "Christmas gift!" and burst into the living room. There in the light of Christmas morning we could see our stockings hanging, with mysterious knobbles sticking out all over them.

How thrilling it was to run fingers down those knobbles and to know they were placed there by a wondrous saint who came down the chimney in the still watches of the Christmas night!

We dived into the depths of the stockings and Christmas day had begun!

—The Des Moines Register, 1943

"We'll sing 'O Little Town of Bethlehem' again, and
this time without the 'Bah! Humbug'!"

\* \* \* Mildred Freburg Berry

# Memories of a Swedish Christmas

 EMORIES OF CHRISTMAS in Scandinavia. Yes, these I have, but there are earlier, more deeply set memories, not of Christmases spent in Scandinavia, but of a Scandinavian Christmas—Christmas on a farm in northern Iowa. Because we lived in a German community we were American in thought and speech for eleven months of the year. But December was different. We became residents again, in everything but fact, of Ivetofta Parish, Sweden.

It was not easy on that farm in Iowa to make such a transformation. Lutfisk, herring, lingonberries, and cardamom seed—all must be ordered at least a month in advance from the big city of Fort Dodge; the dried lutfisk to soak in great tubs of lime water in the cellar, herring to be pickled in vinegar and spices. Biscuits, with glossy egg-topping, were not biscuits without cardamom. What a wonderfully sweet, savory smell: cardamom! Actually they did not remain long in their biscuit state for many were cut in halves and roasted for hours in long, shallow black pans. Enough *skorpa* for all the morning coffees of the Holidays. From the first week in December a veritable olfactory pandemonium reigned in the kitchen. It was a mixture of Christmas sausage (*fläskkorv*), pickled herring (*inlagd sill*), head cheese (*pressylta*), Swedish brown beans (*bruna bönor*), rye, spiced and yeast bread, twists (*kringlor*), and spice cookies (*pepparkakor*). Yet in the end, the smell of cardamom pervaded all. We young fry loved to be there and willingly took on all the dull tasks of beating eggs, grinding meat, stirring sauces, creaming butter and sugar—just to maintain our rights of domain, scarcely eminent and very hard won.

Christmas Eve festivities really began in our family shortly after noon with the traditional visit to the kitchen where we all would "dip in the kettle" (*doppa i gryta*), with a chunk of dark or coarse white bread, to taste the good juices of the Christmas ham (*Julskinka*). In my memory it seemed to precede directly the decoration of the tree, and that was done always behind closed doors by my parents and my older sisters.

The front parlor had been closed since the advent of cold weather, but now the great hard-coal stove with its nickel trimming had been polished and set up. Red folding bells, made of honeycomb tissue paper, were hung in windows and doorways. Father cut pine boughs, small ones, to lay before the outside doors. And then on the morning of Christmas Eve the tree was unloaded. No long-needled balsam, this—but a dark green spruce, compact, thick. We had no strings of electric lights; we had something better: short, white twisted candles which were set in holders. After *doppa i gryta*, my parents and my older sisters went into the front parlor and closed the door.

By four o'clock of Christmas Eve all was ready. My older sisters had taken out the cloth curlers from the hair of us young fry, fixed our hair ribbons and tied our sashes around our finest blue woolpoplin dresses. Smorgasbord was ready! The first course, to be sure, was lutfisk and boiled potatoes. (Although we were served mustard sauce with it, a custom in Skane only, the majority of Swedish people use butter and white sauce.) Then we returned to the board to feast our eyes upon delicacies we would not see again until the next Christmas: the decorated Christmas ham (always in the center of the table), breads and cheeses, sausage, head cheese, brown beans, pickled herring and beets, rice pudding (served hot with cinnamon sugar and butter), pepparkakor and almond patties and finally that most wonderful of all desserts, cheese (*ostkaka*)—a Christmas dessert served mainly in southern Sweden. (Was its taste enhanced by the fact that it took the better part of two days to prepare?)

The climax of my earliest memory of Christmas Eve is the opening of the parlor door. The tree stood in the middle of the room. I saw nothing else for a long while except those flickering, sputtering candles on the tree, a fantastic beauty, a heaven-tree with its silver star at the top leading straight to Heaven—or so I thought. Slowly I realized that there were others in the room. Mother was at the organ; the Swedish song books open, and Father was holding the lamp over the music. The older girls could come in on the choruses; we younger ones just pretended. The hymns were over, and then came the jolly songs which Father loved. We liked them, too, but Mother, I suspect, did not quite approve. Maybe they were songs appropriate only for the dance and clink of the glass. At any rate we always wound up with "Och nu är det Jul igen" (And Now it is Christmas Again), although we didn't understand a word of the song. We marched around the tree, singing less boisterously as the tree once again embraced us.

I was never very sure that Father slept at all that night, for long before the sky lightened, we could hear his slippers flap upon the stairs; he was bringing Mother her coffee. Oh, it was a brooding darkness in which we made ready for the Julotta service! Clammy, icy clothes: it was easier if one got into them hurricdly; and then there was always the problem of making our white ribbed stockings fit without undulant ridges over those long flannels.

Father in coonskin "pels" and black fur cap stood outside by the sleigh, reins in hand, talking to Hans, the hired man. He had fed the bays an extra ration of oats that morning; Hans was Swedish, too, and knew that all animals must have a feast on Christmas Day. He had made the sleigh ready with straw and blankets. We children were already in, kneeling on the blankets. "Take care you don't put your overshoes against our coats," our older sisters warned. Finally Mother, who had a great brown fur cape, muff, and a velvet hat with plumes, emerged. We were off for Julotta. It was a creaking cold pre-dawn. The moon and stars somehow seemed to be very close. One could almost touch the sky—if one tried. The only sounds to break the whiteness and stillness which lay everywhere were the harness bells—a gentle, light sound—and the squeaking of the snow as the runners slid over it. The whiteness seemed sometimes—if there were no lights in the farm houses—like a never-ending gray mist. Once we passed a house close to the road; the isinglass belly of the hardcoal stove shone red through the window; it looked warm and inviting. We rode in silence the six miles except when Mother said quietly, "In Ivetofta there were flares on every fence post to guide us to church on Christmas morning." This was one custom she had not been able to perpetuate here in America.

Then the church appeared. The gray mist suddenly vanished. The light from the tall arched windows spilled out over the snow. Father drove the horses into the hitching stall. He turned to us. His eyebrows and mustache were white with frost. The horses' flanks were covered with rime. We moved, stiff-kneed, with Mother to the church door. Father stayed behind to blanket the horses. In every window there were three candles. The tree was much grander than any I had seen, and its candle flames—myriads of them—seemed to be nodding politely but with restraint to each other. Occasionally one would wag and sputter, but generally they only bowed like the communicants, a polite nod, and then raised their heads as if they, too, were waiting— waiting for the child.

I cannot explain how a sight or a sound, scarce thought of for decades, suddenly impinges upon one with startling vividness. But it does. This moment I can hear the organ swell to the anthem, "Var Hälsad Sköna Morgonstund," (*We Greet Thee, Beautiful Morning Hour*) and, less vividly, in the recessional. What happened in between I do not recall. As we moved down the aisle, the world had changed. The primeval darkness which had lain outside the high windows had gone. The eastern sky was gold and red and blue. Christmas morn: the light had come!

—*Palimpsest*, January 1978

* * * Katherine Buxbaum

# A Festival of Lights

HE TWO great festivals of the Christian year have been so cherished by Moravians that a whole fabric of traditional practices peculiar to the sect has been woven around these seasons. In matters like these we did not mind at all being "different," but gladly laid hold of the inheritance that was ours.

Christmas in the Lapham neighborhood really began with the baking of the cookies. Early in December people began speaking for the cooky cutters. A clever tinsmith back in Ohio had made a specialty of turning them out in fancy shapes, birds, stars, Christmas trees, and a dozen different animal shapes, including a reindeer, whose outlines were the despair of amateur cooky bakers and the triumph of those expert ones who could turn out crisp, thin reindeer with all their horns intact. Housewives borrowed freely and cheerfully lent the cutters; non-Moravian families made the cookies, too; and when the cutters passed on to the next baker they were always accompanied by a sample of the batch. We grew to be connoisseurs of cookies; Mrs. Niedermeier's were the thinnest—a great distinction—but were almost too "brickle." Mrs. Thaeler's were just right; she spared neither shortening nor spice, and balanced amounts of molasses and sugar to a nicety. Since the recipe was in terms of quarts and pounds, no wonder the yield was prodigious. A peck measure full of "shapes" was a commonplace in the household.

There was another mystery with which a few of the initiated were busy during December. The making of candles for the Christmas Eve service was the special prerogative of the oldest women in the congregation, the pioneer mothers who had made candles for home use long before lamps were common. They took great pride in their product, a perfect candle made in the molds they had brought with them to the West. How patiently they coaxed the string that was the wick down through the small hole in the end of the mold, and what pains they took to get the candles out clean and whole and shapely. Then each one must be trimmed with a little petticoat of frilled paper, to catch the wax that would run down the side when the candle was lighted. I speak of what I later learned to know of the process. As children we saw only the finished product, and although we had it each year it was always a new and beautiful surprise.

Adults might pretend that all this fuss over cookies and candles was for the children; as a matter of fact they were expressing themselves in these creative enterprises. It was the same with decorating the church, only this time it was the younger people who claimed their prerogative. Let the old folks and the children stay out of this, especially the children. They were not to see the decorations until the supreme moment of Christmas Eve itself.

On the afternoon of the twenty-third the young men would meet at the cemetery to cut the green that would be needed and bring them up to the church lawn. This was an exciting event, as pines were rare in our section, and besides there is something festive about the very smell of evergreen in December. Returning from school that afternoon I felt my heart leap at the sight of the jolly pile outside the church, and I longed for the day when I would be one of the important people who should take a hand in the decorating.

When the young men came back in the evening the girls would be there too. Their cheeks glowed with the cold when they unwound their "fascinators." Toes and fingers tingling, they stood around the stove chatting for awhile; then someone would say, "Well, I suppose it will be festoons again." Of course it would be festoons. The Sunday before a committee had been appointed to arrange for decorating, but the basic plan always included ropes of evergreens at the windows and spanning the chandeliers. While the boys brought in the boughs the girls hunted up the carpet warp saved from former years. Then they sat down, two by two and began the business of festoon making. Who sat with whom was very important; and the newest romantic attachment was made public in this way. There was something magnetic about the occasion, as there was about the season itself. Winter brought leisure, for one thing; the relentless drive of farm work slowed up, and people felt relaxed, less matter-of-fact than usual. Christmas was an appropriate time for lovers' avowals. Young men might speak their minds on Christmas Eve, when hearts were tender, and when music and poetry (like that in the Bible) charged with allusions to childhood and the ties of home, made a common meeting ground for thoughts.

It would be almost midnight when they finished. They swept up the scraps of green and stepped back to admire the work of their hands. Now the familiar room seemed altogether transformed. The chill of its Puritan simplicity was softened by this gracious greenness, for festoons had been supplemented by wreaths in each window, and at the front of the room was an evergreen arch under which they had placed the minister's cherished *Putz*, a replica of the Nativity scene, complete with manger, cattle, and approaching Wise Men.

Now on Christmas Eve the children came into their own. The "exercises" were theirs, and they were the usual thing: much singing, and much speaking, solos or in concert. The mistakes were theirs, too: a letter in the Merry Christmas legend held upside down; a verse spoken out of turn; too quick or too tardy an entrance into a dialog, if anything so advanced as a dialog was a program feature. People liked that sort of thing, but the costuming was the despair of those who coached the children. How, for instance, could a little girl who wore red flannels be appropriately dressed as an angel? We had no dressing room, and even if we had had one, it would have been risking health to make all the changes a thin summer dress would require! To dress boys as shepherds was another problem. In later years bath robes solved that one. The program committee felt reasonably sure that the Orientals wore bath robes or something very similar.

In all our entertainment there was no mention of Santa Claus. And the Christmas tree, if we had one, was just the tree itself, a symbol, as its inspired chooser, St. Boniface or someone else lost to legend, intended it to be. I am glad that our service did not include the practice of public gift giving. One heard of jealousies, heart burnings, rivalries, and boastings in those places where the Joneses sought to outdo their neighbors by putting a larger doll on the tree for their Mary than the Smiths could provide for their daughter. We were all treated alike with gifts from a common fund, and the gifts were only candy, an orange (rare, then) and the precious candle.

This last was treated with appropriate symbolism. There is a

Moravian hymn dedicated to the ceremony of candle passing, the one known as *Morning Star*, beginning:

*Morning Star, O cheering sight,*
*Ere thou cam'st how dark earth's night.*

The opening lines of each stanza are sung as a solo, then repeated by a quartet with the parts in harmony. Our ministers were particular to carry out this detail, and the assignment of the solo part was indeed an honor. Scarcely less of an honor was the privilege of passing the candles. As soon as the first strains of the hymn were heard, everybody watched to see who would come forward to carry the candle boards. It was usually a young married couple; better still an affianced pair. From behind a screen where someone had been busy lighting the tapers, they brought what looked like a tray load of blossoms, and children gave an ecstatic sigh at sight of all those wavering tiny flames. The couple started down the aisle, "he" carrying the board with a show of great caution, while "she" smiling, put the candles into outstretched hands, whispering something gracious, warning children not to get them too close to clothing or hair. All the while the *Morning Star*, which fortunately has many verses, had continued, and the last notes died away only when the last child in the room had received this coveted gift. After this the minister gave a brief talk about the Light of the World, while dreamy eyes looked into the flames, and heads turned so that eyes could see the room alive with candle glow. When we were told to put out our lights, carefully, one row at a time, there was much puffing, and much sniffing for the blended fragrance of wax and evergreen. Then while the smoke wisps faded on the air we rose for the last hymn, *Joy to the World*, and for the benediction. For us it was the climax of the whole Christmas season.

—*Iowa Outpost* 1948

* * * Bess Streeter Aldrich

# Journey Into Christmas

ARGARET STALEY stood at her library window looking out at the familiar elms and the lace-vine arbor. Tonight the trees were snow-crusted, the arbor crystal filigree under the Christmas stars.

Some years Iowa stayed mild all through December, donning her snowsuit only after the holidays. But tonight was a Christmas Eve made to order, as though Mother Nature had supervised the designing and decorating of a silvered stage setting.

Margaret Staley visualized all this perfection, but she knew that the very beauty of the scene brought into sharper contrast the fact that for the first time in her life she was alone on Christmas Eve.

For fifty-nine Christmases she had been surrounded by the people she loved. On this sixtieth, there was no one. For not one of her four children was coming home.

She could remember reading a story like that once, about a mother who was disappointed that no one was coming—and then, just at dusk on Christmas Eve, all the children and the families arrived together to surprise her. But that was a sentimental piece of fiction; this was cold reality.

The reasons for none of the four coming were all good. Three of the reasons were, anyway, she admitted reluctantly. Calling the roll, she went over—for the hundredth time—why each could not make the trip.

Don. That was understandable. Don and Janet, his wife, and

young Ralph in California could not be expected to come half way across the continent every year, and they had been here last Christmas. She herself had visited them the past summer, returning as late as September.

Ruth. Ruth was her career daughter, connected with a children's hospital and vitally important to her post. Long ago she had accepted the fact that Ruth could give her only the fragments from a busy life and never had she begrudged it; indeed, she had felt vicariously a part of her capable daughter's service to humanity.

Jean. Jeanie and her husband, Roy, lived in Chicago. Jeanie was a great family girl and certainly would have come out home, but the two little boys were in quarantine.

Lee. The hurt which she had loyally pushed into the back of her mind jumped out again like an unwanted and willful jack-in-the-box. Lee and his Ann could have come. Living in Oklahoma, not too far away, they could have made the trip if they had wished. Or if it had not been convenient for Lee to leave, she could have gone down there to be with them. *If they had asked her.*

The only time Christmas had been mentioned was in a letter, now several weeks old. Lee had mentioned casually that they were going to have company for Christmas. That would be Ann's folks of course. You mustn't be selfish. You had to remember that there were in-laws to be taken into consideration.

Standing there at the window, looking out at the silver night, she remembered how she once thought the family would always come home. In her younger years she had said complacently, "I know my children. They love their old home and whenever possible they will spend Christmas in it. Of course there will be sickness and other reasons to keep them away at times, but some of the four will always be here." And surprisingly it had been true. Someone had been here every Christmas.

Faintly into her reveries came the far-off sound of bells and she opened the casement window a bit to locate their tinkling. It was the carolers, carrying out the town's traditional singing on Christmas Eve.

She closed the window and drew the drapes, as though unable to bear the night's white beauty and the poignant notes of young voices.

"I'm alone...I'm alone...it's Christmas Eve and I'm alone." Her mind repeated it like some mournful raven with its "nevermore."

Suddenly she caught herself by a figurative grip. "Now, listen," she said to that self which was grieving. "You are not a weak person and you're not neurotic. You have good sense and understanding and even humor at times. How often have you criticized people for this very thing?"

She walked over to the radio and turned it on, but when "*Silent Night. . . Holy Night*" came softly forth, she snapped it off, afraid she would break down and weep like an old Niobe.

"Oh, go on. . .feel sorry for yourself if you want to. Go on. Do it." She smiled again wryly, and knew she was trying to clutch at humor, that straw which more than once had saved her from drowning in troubled waters.

She went over to her desk and got out the four last letters from the children, although she knew their contents thoroughly.

There was the fat one from Don and Janet with young Ralph's hastily scribbled sixth-grade enclosure. They said the poinsettias were up to the back porch roof, that the Christmas parade had been spectacular, and that they would all be thinking of her on Christmas day when they drove to Laguna Beach.

Then the letter from Jeanie. She had been experiencing one of those times which mothers have to expect, but they were over the hump now and although still in quarantine, she thought Bud could be dressed and Larry sit up by Christmas day. They would all miss the annual trip out home but would be thinking of her.

Ruth's letter was a series of disconnected notes written in odd moments at her desk. Almost one could catch a whiff of hospital odors from them. They were filled with plans for the nurses, the carols, the trees for the convalescents, but as always she would think, too, of home and mother on Christmas day.

From Lee and Ann, nothing but that three-, no, *four*-weeks-old letter with its single casual reference to Christmas. There was a package from them under the tree, attractively packed and addressed in Ann's handwriting. It, too, had been here for weeks. But no recent letter. No special. No wire. No "We will be thinking of you" as the others had written. She tried to push the hurt back and close the lid on it, but she could not forget it was there.

She put the letters away and went into the living room. It looked as big as Grand Central Station. Last year there had been eleven sitting in these chairs which tonight were as empty as her heart. Half ashamed at her childishness in trying to create an illusion, she began pulling them out to form the semicircle of last year when the big tree had been its pivotal point. She could even recall where each had sat that morning at the opening of the gifts. Jeanie and Bud on the davenport, Ruth curled up on the hassock, Ann and Lee side by side in the big blue chairs—and on around the circle.

She had to smile again to remember the red rocking-chair which she brought from the storeroom for young Larry. It had been her own little rocker and was fifty-eight years old. A brown tidy hung limply on its cane back, an old-fashioned piece worked in cross-stitch, the faded red letters reading: FOR MARGARET. Larry had squeezed into it, but when his name was called and he rose excitedly to get his first present, the chair rose with him and they had to pry him out of it and one of the chair's arms cracked. There had been so much hilarious laughter where tonight was only silence. And silence can be so very much louder than noise.

With the chairs forming their ghost-like semi-circle beside her, she turned her own around to the fireplace and sat down to give herself the pleasure and the pain of remembering old Christmases. Swiftly her mind traversed the years, darting from one long gone holiday season to another.

The Christmas before Don was born she and John were in their first new home. They had been very happy that year, just the two of them; so happy in fact that she had felt almost conscience stricken to think she could be contented without her own old family at holiday time. Why, she thought suddenly, that was the way Lee was feeling now, and she could not help a twinge of jealousy at the parting of the ways.

Then Don's first Christmas when he was eleven months old. After these thirty-six years she could still remember how he clutched a big glass marble and would not notice anything else. Strange how such small details stayed in one's mind.

The Christmas before Jeanie was born, when she did not go out to shop, but sent for her gifts by mail, so that the opening of them was almost as much a surprise to her as to the recipients.

Then there was the whooping-cough Christmas, with the house full of medicated steam and all four youngsters dancing and whooping spasmodically around the tree like so many little Indians.

There was the time she bought the big doll for Ruth and when it proved to have a large paint blemish on its leg, she wanted to return it for a perfect one. But Ruth would not hear of it and made neat little bandages for the leg as though it were a wound. It was the first she ever noticed Ruth's nursing instincts.

Dozens of memories flocked to her mind. There had not always been happy holidays. Some of them were immeasurably sad. Darkest of all was the one after John's death, with the children trying to carry out cheerfully the old family customs, knowing that it was what Dad would have wanted. But even in the troubled days there had been warm companionship to share the burden—not this icy loneliness.

For a few moments she sat, unmoving, lost in the memory of that time, then roused herself to continue her mental journeying.

Soon after that dark one, Christmas was no longer a childish affair. Gifts suddenly ceased to be skates and hockey-sticks and became sorority party dresses and fraternity rings, and the house was full of young people home for vacation. Then the first marriage and Don's Janet was added to the circle, then Jeanie brought Roy into it. In time the first grandson. . .and another. . .and a third—all the youthful pleasure of the older members of the family renewed through the children's eyes.

Then came that Christmas when the blast of the ships in their harbor had sent its detonations here into this very living room, as into every one in the country. And though all were here and tried to be natural and merry, only the children were free from forebodings of what the next year would bring. And it brought many changes: Don with his Reserves, Roy enlisting in the Navy, Lee in the Army. That was the year they expected Lee home from the nearby camp. His presents were under the tree and the Christmas Eve dinner ready, only to have him phone that his leave had been cancelled, so that the disappointment was keener than if they had not expected him at all.

Then those dark holiday times with all three boys overseas and Jean and the babies living here at home. Ruth in uniform, coming for one Christmas, calm and clear-eyed as always, realizing perhaps more than the others that at home or abroad, waking or sleeping, Death holds us always in the hollow of his hand.

Then the clouds beginning to lift and, one by one, all coming back, Lee the last to arrive. And that grand reunion of last year after all the separations and the fears. All safe. All home. The warm touch of the hand and the welcoming embrace. Pretty Ann added to the circle. The decorating of the tree. The lights in the window. The darting in and out for last minute gift wrapping. The favorite recipes. Old songs resung. Old family jokes retold. Old laughter renewed. In joy and humility she had said, "My cup runneth over."

Recalling all this, she again grew stern with herself. How could one ask for anything more after that safe return and perfect reunion? But the contrast between then and tonight was too great. All her hopes had ended in loneliness. All her fears of approaching age had become true. One could not help the deep depression. The head may tell the heart all sorts of sensible things, but at Christmastime the heart is stronger.

She sat for a long time in front of the fire which had not warmed her. She had been on a long emotional journey and it had left her tired and spent.

From the library, loud and brazen, the phone rang. It startled her for she had never outgrown her fear of a late call. With her usual trepidation she hastened to answer. There was some delay, a far off operator's voice, and then Lee.

"That you, Mother?"

"Yes, Lee, yes. How are you?"

"Fine. Did Jeanie come?"

"No, the boys are still quarantined."

"Ruth?"

"No."

"You there alone?"

"Yes."

"Gosh, that's too bad on the old family night. Well, cheer up. I've got news for you. Our company came. She weighs seven pounds and fourteen ounces."

"What...what did you say, Lee?"

"Our daughter arrived, Mom. Four hours ago. I waited at the hospital to see that Ann was all right."

"Why, Lee...you never told...we never knew..."

"It was Ann's idea of a good joke. And listen...we named her Margaret...for you, Mother. Do you like it?"

"Why, yes...yes, I do like it, Lee."

There was more, sometimes both talking at once and having to repeat. Then Lee saying, "We were wondering if you could come down in a couple of weeks. Ann thinks she'd like to have an old hand at the business around. Can you arrange it?"

"Oh, yes, Lee...I'm sure I could."

"Good. Well, I'll hang up now. Spent enough on my call ...have to save my money to send Margaret to college. Be seeing you."

"*Lee*..." In those last seconds she wanted desperately to put into words all the things her heart was saying. But you cannot put the thoughts garnered from a life of love and service into a sentence. So she only said: "Be a good dad, Lee. Be as good a dad as..." She broke off, but he understood.

"I know...I'll try. Merry Christmas, Mom."

"Merry Christmas, Lee."

She put down the receiver and walked into the living room, walked briskly as though to tell her news, her heart beating with pleasant excitement. The semicircle of chairs confronted her. With physical sight she saw their emptiness. But, born of love and imagination, they were all occupied as plainly as ever eyes had seen them. She had a warm sense of companionship. The house seemed alive with humans. How could they be so real? She swept the circle with that second sight which had been given her. Don over there...Ruth on the hassock...Jeanie on the davenport...Lee and Ann in the big blue chairs...

Suddenly she turned and walked hurriedly down the hall to the closet and came back with the little red chair. She pushed the two blue chairs apart and set the battered rocker between them. On the back hung the old brown tidy with its red cross-stitching: FOR MARGARET.

She smiled at it happily. All her numbness of spirit had vanished, her loneliness gone. This was a good Christmas. Why, this was one of the best Christmases she ever had!

She felt a sudden desire to go back to the library, to look out at the silvery garden and up to the stars. That bright one up there—it must be the one that stops over all cradles...

Faintly she could hear bells and voices. That would be the young crowd coming back from their caroling, so she opened the window again.

> *Oh, little town of Bethlehem,*
> *How still we see thee lie...*

The words came clearly across the starlit snow, singing themselves into her consciousness with a personal message:

> *Yet in thy dark streets shineth*
> *The everlasting light*
> *The hopes and fears of all the years*
> *Are met in thee tonight.*

The hopes and fears of all the years! She felt the old Christmas lift of the heart, that thankfulness and joy she had always experienced when the children were all together...all well...all home.

"My cup runneth over."

At the door of the living room she paused to turn off the lights. Without looking back toward the circle of chairs, so there might come no disillusion, she said over her shoulder:

"Good-night, children. Merry Christmas. See you early in the morning."

* * * Eva Marie Noé

# Amana Christmas

T'S BEEN snowing most of the day. Gently and ever so softly, the sparkling snow flakes have drifted down to the earth, until all the world around is glistening and white and—breathless—almost as if it were waiting for something wonderful to happen! If you stand very still in the snow, you can almost hear the branches sigh and creak in the cold night air, with their heavy burdens of snow and ice.

And now, let's turn back the pages of memory and peek though the frosty windows of a modest home, and, through the eyes of a child, see how a certain Amana family celebrates Christmas.

Happy and busy days have preceded this great day. Mother is occupied with the baking of delicious Christmas Stollen, and the heavenly fragrance of Lebkuchen (small cakes) and Pfeffernüsse (gingerbread cookies) fills the house. The children are gathered around the warm woodburning stove, talking excitedly about Sankt Nikolaus, and what he might bring good boys and girls. Also is mentioned, in hushed and anxious whispers, the old story of the little boy who had been so naughty that not even one toy had been left for him under the tree, only a long, black stick!

The time is about five o'clock, the kerosene lamps are not lighted as yet. Not until it is really dark, for there is no reason to waste the precious kerosene. You see, these were a thrifty people, and each family was given just so much kerosene a week, which was carried on foot, in a can with a long spout from the General Store. What an argument we used to have, trying to figure out whose turn it was to walk up to the store and use the smelly old pump.

There comes that lovely time between dusk and nightfall, which only those of you who have grown up with the kerosene lamp can understand. There is no light in the room except the comforting glow of the fat bellied stove. This is always a quiet, sensitive, almost a "holy" time, when one is apt to whisper, and speak of tender things. When grandmothers tell stories of long ago to wide-eyed pigtailed little girls who dream dreams. Quarrels of the day are forgotten and the world is a lovely, mystic place in the deepening twilight.

It was then when our mother would gently say, "Children, you must be sure to look this holy night at the deep, deep red of the sky," (made more so by the darkness of the room and the snow outside). She would continue, "My, my, how busy those little angels must be tonight, baking cookies for the Christkindlein, the Christ Child!" And then the children would gaze with wonder at the sky and try to imagine how many kinds and shapes of cookies they were baking, and whether angel cookies in heaven were any different from their own right here on earth. This precious little story was always told the children around Christmas, and to this day the sight of a lovely deep red sky brings back childhood memories.

It was at such times that the children would sing songs, such as the happy, joyful song, "Ihr Kinderlein, kommet, o kommet doch all," "Oh, come little Children, come one, come all, come to the manger in Bethlehem's stall."

Christmas in those days was truly a happy, carefree time, without the stress and strain of our present day. There was not the problem of finding parking places, then dashing from store to store to find suitable gifts for everyone, and then home again to relieve the baby sitter. Here there were always plenty of sitters, either a grandmother or some other relative lived nearby. Often the families, including the grandparents, lived together in one large house. As for parking problems, you see there were no cars, and everyone walked to the one General Store. This wonderful place, the General Store, was truly a dream come true. It was an exciting day when it was told around, via the grapevine, that the Christmas candy had been put out! There were hard candies, assorted in large wooden buckets, sold by the pound, old fashioned chocolate drops in tall glass jars, as well as chocolate mice, with strings for their tails!

There was really no particular rush, since there was only the one store, and the choice of gifts was not great. Yet, there was that wonderful sort of excitement, Christmas was close by, and it was the loveliest time of the year.

As for the rush of getting Christmas cards off, this was simple, since there were no fancy cards to be had at the Store, and anyway, no one had money for such luxuries. Sometimes the children would exchange little pictures of angels or santas, or post cards could be purchased for a few pennies. Pictures were often given with the purchase of a spool of thread.

However, there was a much more delightful custom these simple people had. It was the friendly, heartwarming custom of shaking hands as one passed along the street, and calling out with a cheery, "Fröhliche Weihnachten," or on New Year's morning, "Ein gluckliches Neues Jahr." The children were taught to stop for a moment whenever a church elder came along, and to politely shake his hand. This recalls to my mind one particular elder. He was the man who made all the little lamp shades for the community—the lamp shades which sat on the top of the glass chimneys of the kerosene lamps. This elder was a chubby, gentle little man, and his hand was soft and his handshake very limp. Whenever we could escape shaking his hand we would do it, even if it meant crossing the street and going up the other side! Now in payment for making these shades (no one of course was paid in money), this little man more or less expected a jar of homemade jam, and, I remember, it was whispered about that he was so fond of jam that he didn't spread it on his bread as most people do, but ate it with a spoon right out of the jar!

In contrast, I remember another elder. He was tall, slender and dark. He was a quiet man with gentle ways, a serious, kindly face, and, I remember—he had a black beard. Whenever I shook hands with him, I was awed by him, and as a small child he reminded me of pictures I had seen of Jesus. His name happened to be Abraham Noé, grandfather of my husband, and one of the leaders of the community.

The stocking hang-up nights will never be forgotten. This was usually done several weeks before Christmas. We still observe this delightful custom in our home. Of course we hang our stockings on our fireplace, and they are bright, red, pretty stockings. However, in those days we had no fireplaces, but instead we looped our stockings over the metal holders which held back the plain white curtains, or we used the posters of the old walnut beds for the same purpose. The stockings, in contrast, were the never-to-be forgotten, long, black, itchy wool stockings! These might contain nuts, candy-mice, or even possibly an orange, with a sun-kist stamped on it, which was truly a treat. I can still see my younger brother, he would hang up his stockings every single night, and each time it was empty (and I can assure you that it was empty more times than it was full), he would slap that long black stocking on his poster bed as hard as he could in anger, until it looked like a shapeless black rope!

Well, finally, the great day is here, and we find the family gathered around the dining room table, with its red and white checkered table cloth, kerosene lamps burning brightly, wicks freshly trimmed, and glass chimneys shining with an extra-special luster! The family, father and mother, two boys and two girls. The mother is bustling about busy with the food. The children are making a brave attempt to eat at least some of the food on their plates, for food, indeed, this night is scarcely noticed by the children. Why, mother might have served the much hated 'Froschaugen Suppe,' yes, even this would have been gulped down without complaint. To explain to you the ingredients of this most succulent dish, it was simply a thin meat broth, with the old-fashioned large, round tapioca floating around in it. The translation of 'Froschaugen Suppe' is 'Frogeyes Soup,' the tapioca looking for all the world like glassy frog eyes staring right up at you!

Suddenly the little dark-haired girl finds it impossible to contain herself any longer. All her pent-up excitement needs to be expressed in some way. She quickly climbs on a chair, stands up, and in a childish voice, joyfully sings—

> O Tannenbaum, O Tannenbaum
> wie treu sind deine Blätter!
> Du grunst nicht nur zur Sommerzeit,
> nein, auch im Winter, wenn es schneit.
> O Tannenbaum, O Tannenbaum,
> wie treu sind deine Blätter!

The song is ended, and with a start the child realizes what she has done and where she is—at the DINNER TABLE. Too much talking at the table, and certainly singing, was frowned upon. "We come to the table to eat, not to talk," was always the remark. Strict as the rules were and stern as the father was, he does not have the heart to scold the exuberant little girl, for after all this is Christmas Eve!

Father is heartily partaking of his food, in fact, the children feel he is overdoing it a bit, just to try their patience. On his plate is his favorite meat, Bratwurst (pork sausage), home made in the local butcher shop and simmered just long enough to make the skin sort-of-blown-up and squishy like. Mashed potatoes, a common dish to you, but very special to these people, for it takes milk and butter to make them taste good. Milk and butter are rationed to each family. Well, finally he is finished, and pushing back his chair, remarks what a wonderful meal he has enjoyed.

Remember, now, the children have not had even a glimpse of the Christmas tree. All day long the parlor has been tightly locked and dark green shades pulled down. Eager ears are pressed to the door, and vain attempts are made to peek through the keyhole, but alas, the large key is safely in the lock on the other side, and any peeking is hopeless!

Suddenly Father and Mother seem to vanish, the oldest of the girls takes over and attempts to keep the smaller children quiet. Hearts are close to the bursting point, and the children listen intently for a certain well-known voice. Listen! There it is, loud, heavy footsteps, a tinkling of bells and a hearty voice booming forth with "Fröhliche Weihnachten," then the slamming of the front door. It is of course Sankt Nikolaus leaving in his own typical fashion.

The children line up, 'the youngest one first' was always the way it was.

Then as if by magic, the closed door is flung open, and there it is, in all its glory, der Weinacht Baum, the Christmas tree looking like Heaven itself must look!

There is the oval table with the claw legs, and all the leaves put in it to make it nice and big. A pure white linen table cloth, and in the middle of the table is the Christmas tree, which Father had cut only a day ago from the Schulwald, the School Grove or Forest (the trees having been planted by the school children of the village long years ago in the 1880s). Around the tree is a white picket fence, which someone had lovingly carved by hand. Inside the fence is the manger scene and little wooden sheep, nestled all about.

The tree sparkles with lights, not electric lights, but candles, red, green, pink, yellow and white, the old twisted kind, and there it is, that special sort-of-fragrance, that of burning candles and evergreens

Amana boy and girl with Christmas gifts

all through the house.

The children have their own particular places at the table. There are no fancily wrapped packages, for the gifts are placed in plain sight under the tree, and you see at a glance whether the gift you want most is there or not.

Dolls, dressed in hand-made clothes, doll beds made of solid walnut, sleds and doll houses created by a carpenter in the village. There are hand-knit mittens, German picture books, pretty cups and saucers and even a silver teaspoon with the child's name on it.

At each child's place is a dish of colored popcorn, nuts, candy, as well as molasses and hickory nut cookies. It is also the duty of the children to watch carefully the candles at their own particular place at the table, in case the flame comes too close to a pine branch. Occasionally, there was a small fire, which always created great excitement, and was only too gladly put out by,—more squirting than was needed, with a squirt gun the boys had handy. A pail of water was always kept under the table for a real emergency.

When finally all the excitement is over, a feeling of sadness comes to the heart of the little dark-haired girl, for now that Christmas has come and gone, she knows that she will have to wait another long year before this glorious moment will come again. She comforts herself with the child-like thought that the precious Christkindlein will remain with her always!

And now it is bedtime—reluctantly the little girls rock their dolls to sleep, and with a kiss, reassure their old dolls that they are still their favorites. The boys take a last quick turn on their fiery hobby horse with the swishing tail. To end the most beautiful evening of the whole year, the children and parents join in singing together, with the mother's lovely voice leading, the old beloved German Christmas song,

*Stille Nacht, heilige Nacht!*
*Alles schläft, einsam wacht*
*Nur das traute hochheilige Paar,*
*Holder Knabe im lockigen Haar,*
*Schlaf in himmlischer Ruh,*
*Schlaf in himmlischer Ruh.*

—*The Iowan* Winter, 1970

* * * James Whitcomb Riley

# His Christmas Sled

I WATCH him with his Christmas sled;
 He hitches on behind
A passing sleigh, with glad hooray,
 And whistles down the wind;
He hears the horses champ their bits,
 And bells that jingle-jingle—
You Woolly Cap! you Scarlet Mitts!
 You miniature "Kriss Kringle!"

He winks at twinklings of the frost,
 And on his airy race,
Its tingles beat to redder heat
 The rapture of his face:—
The colder, keener is the air,
 The less he cares a feather.
But, there! he's gone! and I gaze on
 The wintriest of weather!

Ah, Youth! still speeding o'er the track
 Where none returns again,
To sigh for you, or cry for you,
 Or die for you were vain.—
And so, speed on! the while I pray
 All nipping frosts forsake you—
Ride still ahead of grief, but may
 All glad things overtake you!

* * * Julie McDonald

# The Lesser Christmas Miracle

T'S EASY for an Iowa child to believe what my Danish grandmother told me—that the farm animals celebrate the birth of Christ with human utterance at midnight on Christmas Eve. I first believed it on a farm near Fiscus, and it flowed like a sweet undercurrent beneath the many preparations for the holiday.

A piece had to be learned for the Christmas program at Merrill's Grove Baptist church, and I was admonished not to twist the hem of my skirt to immodest heights while delivering it. I performed without a lapse of memory and left my hemline alone, and when the program was over, we all got brown paper bags filled with hard candy. The bumpy raspberries with soft centers were my favorites, but I also admired the small rounds with a flower that remained visible until the candy was sucked to a sliver.

I had plans to visit the barn at midnight to hear what the cattle had to say to each other, but I kept them to myself, sensing that I would be thwarted should anyone find out. The paradoxically soft and stark light of the kerosene lamps shone on the clock face I could not yet read, and I asked again and again, "Is it midnight yet?" I had never experienced a midnight, and that prospect plus talking animals was almost too much excitement to bear.

My parents spoke of Santa Claus, which presented a problem. If I went to the barn at midnight to listen to the animals, Santa Claus would have to wait to bring my presents, and he might not be able to work me into his route. What to do?

Exhaustion solved my dilemma. I awoke in my own bed in the cold light of Christmas morning and hurried to the dining room to see what Santa had brought with no more than a fleeting regret about missing the animal conversation. There would be other years, other midnights. Now there was the joy of a small table painted bright orange and a sack of peanuts in the shell. The gifts seemed wonderful to me, and I had no notion of the thought and struggle that went into them in that Depression year. For years I did not know that my father made the table from an apple box, a broomstick and the core of a linoleum roll or that finding a few cents to buy peanuts involved looking through pockets and old purses for forgotten coins.

Later in the morning I went to the barn, hoping that the cattle still might have the power to speak, but they didn't. I had missed the moment, and now they only chewed and exhaled their grain-sweet breath in my face. "I'll come next year," I said, but I never did. That was my last Christmas on the farm and my father's last Christmas on earth. We moved to town.

In Harlan, Christmas meant colored lights strung from the Shelby County courthouse like a brilliant spider web, blue electric candles in Aunt Mary's window, and in Grandma's house (where we were living), a Christmas tree with wax candles—so lovely and so dangerous. We walked the streets of the town and admired the electric lights in other peoples' windows.

There were other Christmases in other houses, and for our family, hard times persisted, but they didn't seem so hard at the time. One year when we couldn't afford a Christmas tree, we cut a bough from the huge pine on the family cemetery plot and thrust it into a crock of sand. Then we punctured our fingers stringing popcorn and cranberries and made chains of paper loops to decorate it. The bough smelled as a Christmas tree should, but it also wept resin, recalling its funereal origin. That crying "tree" was banked with the best gifts we could manage, and I recall my delight with a glamorous milk glass flower pot filled with bath salts topped by a shiny and unnatural blue poinsettia.

In town, I could not go to the barn to listen to the animals talking, but I thought of them and wondered what they would say.

Many years later when I had children of my own, we were horse-sitting for my in-laws in Davenport at Christmas, and I was the last one up, filling stockings. As midnight struck with Westminster chimes, I considered going to the stable. I even reached for my coat, but I hung it up again. Mute horses would have stolen something precious from me. This dearest Christmas fancy of an Iowa child was something I wanted to keep, and I have. Surely the miraculous reason for Christmas can support this endearing lesser miracle.

* * * Grace Noll Crowell

# Leisure

I shall attend to my little errands of love
    Early this year,
So that the brief days before Christmas may be
    Unhampered and clear
Of the fever of hurry. The breathless rushing
    That I have known in the past
Shall not possess me. I shall be calm in my soul
    And ready at last
For Christmas — the Mass of Christ — I shall kneel
    And call out his name;
I shall have leisure — I shall go out alone
    From my roof and my door;
I shall not miss the silver silence of stars
    As I have before;
And oh, perhaps — if I stand there very still
    And very long,
I shall hear what the clamor of living has kept from me —
    The angel's song.

* * * Eugene Field

# Jest 'Fore Christmas

Father calls me William, sister calls me Will,
Mother calls me Willie, but the fellers call me Bill!
Mighty glad I ain't a girl—ruther be a boy,
Without them sashes, curls an' things that's worn by Fauntleroy!
Love to chawnk green apples an' go swimmin' in the lake—
Hate to take the castor-ile they give for bellyache!
'Most all the time the whole year round, there ain't no flies on me,
But jest 'fore Christmas I'm as good as I kin be!

Got a yeller dog named Sport, sick him on the cat;
First thing she knows she doesn't know where she is at!
Got a clipper sled, an' when us kids goes out to slide,
'Long comes the grocery cart, and we all hook a ride!
But sometimes when the grocery man is worrited and cross,
He reaches at us with his whip, an' larrups up his hoss,
An' then I laugh and holler, "Oh, ye never teched *me!*"
But jest 'fore Christmas I'm as good as I kin be!

Gran'ma says she hopes that when I git to be a man,
I'll be a missionarer like her oldest brother, Dan,
As was et up by the cannibuls that lives in Ceylon's Isle,
Where every prospeck pleases, and only man is vile!
But gran'ma she has never been to see a Wild West show,
Nor read the life of Daniel Boone, or else I guess she'd know
That Buff'lo Bill an' cowboys is good enough for me!
*Excep'* jest 'fore Christmas, when I'm good as I kin be!

And then old Sport he hangs around, so solemnlike and still,
His eyes they seem a-sayin': "What's the matter, little Bill?"
The old cat sneaks down off her perch an' wonders what's become
Of them two enemies of hern that used to make things hum!
But I am so perlite an' tend so ernestly to biz,
That mother says to father: "How improved our Willie is!"
But father, having been a boy hisself, suspicions me
When, jest 'fore Christmas, I'm as good as I kin be!"

For Christmas, with its lots an' lots of candies, cakes, an' toys,
Was made, they say, for proper kids, an' not for naughty boys;
So wash yer face and bresh yer hair, and mind yer p's and q's,
And don't bust out yer pantaloons, and don't wear out yer shoes;
Say "Yessum" to the ladies, and "Yessur" to the men,
And when they's company, don't pass yer plate for pie again;
But thinkin' of the things yer'd like to see upon that tree,
Jest 'fore Christmas be as good as yer kin be!

* * * Hadley Read

# Garden Center
# Christmas Program

Murmuring voices fade.
A quiet hush invades the room.
It now becomes
      a center for the performing arts.

Three borrowed muslin sheets
      starched fresh and ironed smooth
united now as one with safety pins
curtain off from view the center stage.

The house is packed.
The audience awaits.
Proud parents all in gingham gowns and overalls
      sit beneath streamers made of crepe.

Out in the hall
      beside the hanging coats and caps
the cast of famous acting stars
silently rehearse their lines
      and dry their sweaty hands.

The time has come.
No turning back,
Inside the house lights dim
      as borrowed lamps are turned down low.
The actors put aside their fright.

The Garden Center Christmas program now begins
with sixteen off-key voices singing.
　　　　　"Silent Night."

# The Christmas Season

## The Revelation

Some modern parents think it wrong
to let kids when they're young
believe in Santa Claus
and then reveal the truth a little later on.
I don't know the pros and cons of that.
But I believed in old Saint Nick
　　　　　　　　when I was growing up
and never thought it did much harm.
I even thought it sort of fun
when I found out that Santa Claus
　　　　　　　　was really Dad and Mom.
Here's how it came about.
My older brother
　　　　wiser for his extra years
told me he could prove his case
since I was filled with doubt.
So once we went to bed on Christmas Eve
　　　　　　　　we stayed awake.
Then like quiet elves
we saw the truth unfold below
　　　　as we watched through the chimney grate.
In actual fact
we played the pretend game an extra year.
We wanted Mom and Dad to have the fun
　　　　　　　　of playing Santa Claus.

## The Dream Book

Wind-up trains complete with tracks.
Cowboy suits with leather chaps.
Model cars and gopher traps.
Erector sets and Tinkertoys.
Tops that spin like gyroscopes.
Fancy saddles for the pony.
Indian bows with twenty arrows.
Pocket knives and fancy watches.

Horseshoe sets and two-head axes.
Flyer sleds and coaster wagons.
Frontier forts you build with matches.
Stocking caps and matching jackets.
Magic sets and pencil boxes.

The fire glows.
Stretched out on the floor
     I lie there warm
          and dream my Christmas dream.
If only everything were free
     as offered in the catalog
put out by Sears Roebuck and Company.

## Mom's Christmas Candy

Rich and full bodied
     languid and sensuous
dusky brown from a thousand suns
tempting with fragrance of other lands
     sweet chocolate
          the essence of vanilla
hot blooded and indolent
moving indifferently into the shallow pan to cool.

The first full batch of fudge is done.
Mom lets us lick the pan.

Prim and proper
        like young girls at their first dance
all alike in white dresses
        innocent and shy
sitting politely in straight rows
waiting
offering sugar-sweet temptation
hidden now in coolness
        behind closed parlor doors.
We have to wait 'till Christmas Day
to have these lovely maidens of divinity
                that Mom has made.

## Christmas Eve

No night could be more special
        more filled with warmth
                more touched with cheer
more vividly remembered now for special things.
Snow creaking in the cold
                as we do chores.
First night stars
        soon joined by millions more
the way it must have been that night
                so long ago.

The kitchen filled with lamplight.
The table set.
The menu just the same
as all the other Christmas Eves before
        and all the ones we'd ever know.
A giant kettle warms atop the kitchen range
        filled half with milk and half with cream
soon joined by oysters Mom pours in
        at least a quart or two
for feasting Christmas Eve on oyster stew.

Hurry now to dress in Sunday best.

The program starts at eight.
We'll miss the Christmas carols if we're late.
The ride to town.
A winter wonderland of falling snow.
We're there.
Everybody stamps their feet
so not to track the damp inside.

From up in front
a mammoth Christmas tree surveys the scene.
Its branches laced with tinsel strands
               and bright red paper chains
and ornaments of every kind
               made by the Ladies Aid.
There's murmured neighbor talk
about those things that neighbors talk about.

The program is about to start.
The church is filled with muffled quietness.
The curtains part to show the manger scene.
Three wise men walk onto the stage.
They're boys we know
               in costumes that their mothers made.
They're joined by little angels dressed in white
All speak their lines
               and then depart relieved.
Their places taken turn by turn
               by others chosen to recite.

The curtains close again.
The program's over for the night.
We wait for what we know will come.
The sound of sleigh bells drawing near.
And then a loud commotion at the door.
A hearty ho ho laugh
and sure enough
there's someone all dressed up like Santa Claus.
The younger kids are sort of scared.
The older ones all think they know
it's neighbor Anderson

with pillows front and rear.
How can they be so sure?
He stops and asks each one if he's been good.
And when the answer's yes
he reaches in his bag
and fishes out a small brown paper bag
filled to the top
with cheap rock Christmas candy.
How could there be in all the world
a nicer gift than that.

The snow has stopped.
The night is colder still.
As we drive home this silent night
there truly is a peace on earth—
          or so at least it seemed
          when we were growing up.

## Christmas Morning

Still dark with night inside our room.
I am awake.
I pull the curtain back and peer outside.
The stars are there
          as bright as when we went to bed.
And yet I'm sure the sky is lighter
                    in the east.
It is a subtle kind of lightness
                    only boys can see
when morning comes to Christmas Day.

I lie there warm and wait.
A teasing pleasure in delay.
My mind plays guessing games.
What will I find when I dash down
          dressed only in my underwear?
There are so many things I've dreamed about.

My brothers move.
They are awake.
We softly talk.

We say we'll wait 'till each one counts
five hundred times real fast
and then we'll make a dash downstairs.
My turn comes last.
I reach four hundred ninety-nine.
With that we toss the covers back and run.
No time to light the lamp
          and anyway it's lighter out.
I see it there
          beneath the stocking with my name.
A giant cardboard box.
I shout out loud.
My heart begins to pound.
I know inside that box
I'll find a brand new wind up train
                    with twenty feet of track.
The dream I dared to dream came true.
Santa Claus is real regardless of his honest name.

## Christmas Day

Chores got done on Christmas Day
          same as any other day I guess.
Cows got milked and cattle fed.
Barns got cleaned and all the rest.
Those things are hazy in my mind.
I find a lot of other things
much easier to recall.

We set the train track up
and ran my train around the figure eight
                    at least a hundred times.
We coasted on the Flyer sled
          my little brother got
and shot my older brother's .22.

We tried on brand-new stocking caps
                    and skated on the pond.
We hitched the horses to the sleigh
and drove to see the Wilson boys

to try out all the gifts they got.

Sometime in early afternoon we headed home
and helped Mom get the Christmas dinner on.
We ate until there wasn't room for more.
Then we pulled our chairs up to the stove
and talked or took a little snooze
until Dad roused us out to help with chores.

That's how it was on Christmas Day.

*—Morning Chores and Other Times Remembered*

# Day Before Christmas

We have been helping with the cake
    And licking out the pan,
And wrapping up our packages
    As neatly as we can.
And we have hung our stockings up
    Beside the open grate,
And now there's nothing more to do
    Except
        To
            Wait!

\* \* \* Marchette Chute

* * * Marjorie Holmes

## Christmas Is My
## Memory Season

HERE IS no more beautiful celebration of Christmas than in that great city which belongs to all of us, Washington, D. C. Each year a different state ships to the nation's capitol its tallest, most magnificent tree. This is erected on the Mall, as the crowning feature of the Pageant of Peace. I have stood there with my children awaiting the thrilling moment when, at the touch of the President's hand, that tree springs into fabulous, living light.

We have sat in the National Cathedral, hearing choirs of trained voices present the Messiah. We have walked the fairyland of lighted streets. We have gazed into the marvels of animation in store windows, depicting the legends and fantasies of the holiday. On rare occasions when the weather was cold enough, our sons have joined the ice skaters who skim below Lincoln's feet on the famous Reflecting Pool. We have toured the White House decked out in all its festive attire. All the skills of professional artists and decorators combine to achieve perfection in this perfect mansion for this perfect holiday.

But we have always stood longest in the foyer where, usually, there stands an old-fashioned, ceiling-high, popcorn- and cookie-trimmed Christmas tree. There are gingerbread men and women too, and quaint and fragile ornaments. There are nuts and fruits and velvet bows such as a mother might have kept in her dresser drawer. There are chains of paper loops like children used to make.

And this, it seems to me, is significant. That in a land of

sophistication and plenty, the truest symbol of Christmas is, after all, an old-fashioned family kind of tree.

It brings back all the Christmases past that I knew as a little girl in Storm Lake, Iowa. It brings back the winter sports that were their glorious preview; the ice skating, the snow battles, the hopping of bobs. An entire new era of delight was ushered in with the first snowfall, and with the freezing of the lake it became an immense reality.

The lake, that vast rolling body of water in which we had frolicked all summer, became forbidden territory soon after Labor Day. Though it continued to rush shoreward with foaming force, we knew that the days of its might were numbered. Winter was watching from behind the gold, then gradually naked trees. Soon the water would lie subdued, the first sheets of ice inching out from the shore. Every day some daring boy would test its surface, racing back at the sounds of cracking. But the cold and certain encroachment was taking place; until one day, after severe nights and several false reports, the word would spread through town: "The lake's frozen over!" And though parents remained doubtful and issued edicts and warnings, the first few figures began taking tentative swings across its glassy expanse.

"Darn fools!" our dad would declare. "You kids aren't setting foot on that ice until we're sure it's *safe.*"

"But it is!" we'd claim. "Old Doc Vanderhoof's been going out every day."

Old Vanderhoof, a retired "horse doctor," was also our local Hans Brinker. Dutch born, a superb skater. Whenever you saw that tubby figure, arms folded, pipe in his mouth, white whiskers blowing, doing his loops and turns, the parents were assured. The ice was safe.

Our skates had been ready for days. Dug from cellar, barn or attic, sharpened, polished, their worn straps tested, tried on repeatedly. "Now take those things off," Mother scolded, as we clumped or wobbled about, "you'll cut the rug, you'll scar the floor." Each year we inherited bigger ones from older brothers and sisters, and passed ours down. Or we traded with the neighbors. Sometimes the purchase of a new pair was not to be avoided, and oh, the thrill of those tough, strong, leathery-smelling straps, the brilliance of the blades. Shoe skates were unheard of. It was important, therefore, to have strong thick-soled shoes for the clamps to clutch.

Once, for my birthday in late September, I asked only for my own brand new ice skates. They seemed unbearably beautiful lying in the box. I'd test their sharpness with a finger, and sometimes, in secret, hold their cold promise against my cheek. The weather seemed unseasonably warm, the wait for their initiation intolerable. Worse, my high-top black shoes with which they were to be worn, were getting thin. By the time the ice and the lovely skates were ready, my shoes were shot. It was a lean year, and new ones were out of the question. I had to suffer the ignominy, after all, of some beaten-up old straps across my toes.

We lived only two blocks from the lake. On Saturdays, and most days after school, we hastened down to The Point, a favorite gathering place. Here a tipsy old green boathouse afforded shelter from the stinging blasts. It was always intensely cold, and though we were lumpy with long underwear, and bundled to the eyebrows in layers of sweaters, jackets, leggings, mufflers, mittens, we huddled in its protection, or drew gratefully toward the great crackling fire that older boys often built among the rocks.

Armed with stubby brooms, the boys would have swept the snow aside for a hockey court. And what blithe young gods they seemed as they smacked the little puck with their store-bought or home-made hockey sticks, laughing, yelling, fighting, with a fierce and joyous abandon; or often gliding swiftly up to see how the girls were getting along.

There was about them a gallantry and kindness absolutely singular to this contact. At home or at school they might ignore us, tease us,

pull our hair or even hit us, but at this gathering upon the ice they became knights in stocking caps and mackinaws. They helped us with our skates; they asked if we were warm enough, and if we weren't they made us go home or sometimes rubbed our hands and feet. They taught the beginners patiently; they steered us about showing us how to skate backward and figure eights. And no matter who it was, even a brother or some dumb neighborhood kid, a sense of our own fledgling womanhood was sweetly roused by their attentiveness. While to have one of the true heroes, say a football player or a town lifeguard, kneel at your feet just to tighten a skate was to fall instantly, madly, hopelessly in love.

The boys never suffered us to join their hockey games. And, true Vikings that they were, girls had no place on their iceboats. They fashioned these magical craft themselves out of two-by-fours hauled home from the lumber yard by sled or coaster wagons. These they nailed together crosswise, and masted with a piece of canvas, or more

likely a mother's bed sheet. The runners and rudders they carved of wood, the runners bladed with strips of metal which were forged and shaped to the purpose by Pat McCabe in his blacksmith shop. We sometimes watched the process, Pat's white teeth flashing in his smoke-blackened face. The glow of his forge lit up the mysterious recesses of his cavern where all manners of interesting objects hung: wagon wheels and horseshoes, pipes and bars and farming tools. There was the smell of hot iron and horses and leather and steam as this skilled and dusky wizard plied his trade.

Perched at front or rear of the boats, or lying flat, the boys steered these fleet ships into vast blue gleaming distances of the lake where only a foolhardy skater dared venture. (There were air holes; every now and then the town was shaken by some skater's shooting into such a hole and being trapped beneath the ice. This was our parents' greatest concern.) But the ice boaters were charmed beings, winged by the wind, flying safe and free.

Boys also fought pitched battles from behind their snow-forts, and here the girls were allowed, if only in the capacity of providing ammunition. Our job was to make the snowballs, and we gloated over our growing stock, much as our mothers proudly counted their canning. A good snowball maker was much in demand. I always envied Ellen Lincoln who was first to be chosen when she trudged out. She fashioned round firm snowballs with the same methodical skill as she turned out loaves of bread for her mother, or a firm creamy platter of fudge. Hers put my leaky, topsided snowballs to shame. An even higher honor was accorded Alberta (Bert) Manfred, a husky girl who knew more about football than most boys, and had such a terrific pitching arm she was not only allowed on the team, she sometimes led the charge.

But for sheer exhilerating delight nothing could equal hitching bobsled rides. With the onset of winter, cars were hoisted onto blocks to protect the tires, and stored away. There were simply no facilities for sweeping the snow-muffled streets. Townspeople walked (or waded) to their destinations; country people traveled by bob. Saturday was the big trading day in town, and consequently the best day for hopping bobs. Farmers approaching Storm Lake by almost any road were met by a swarm of kids, most of them pulling sleds. If you didn't have a sled you hopped on the long wooden runner, and hung onto the wagon box. With a sled you looped its rope over a bolt at the back, or through a brace at its side.

A good natured farmer usually *"Whoa-ed"* his team to a halt so that you could get attached, or he at least slowed down. A mean one, spying the eager contingent, would whip his horses on faster. It was fun to run madly after, trying to catch him anyway. It added to the thrill. Hooking a ride with someone who didn't even suspect you were there was especially exciting, dangerous as it was. He might make a sudden turn or stop and throw you off.

Parents were always issuing futile edicts against the hopping of bobs. Yet they too remembered the thrill of hopping belly-flat upon a sled that went whistling and bouncing across the crusty and glittering ground—here bumpy, here glass-smooth, here stained mustard-yellow, here grayly tramped, here purest shining white.... While up front there was the steady plocking rhythm of the horses' hooves, the jingle of harness, the creak and rattle of the wagon box, while sometimes wisps of straw flew back like pinfeathers from angel wings.

Clutching the wooden rudders of our sleds, we steered, avoiding the deeper ruts; and rounding a corner, trying not to swing too far to the side. You could lose your grip, skid off, hit a curb, a lamp post, or be hurled into the path of an oncoming team. Thus the perils, tempering our pleasure, yet enhancing it.

Bobsleds were great to ride in too, out to Grandpa Holmes' or an uncle's, snuggled down inside the tickling straw. We made tents of the scratchy, raw-smelling horse blankets, and burrowed down like groundhogs, cozy and squirming, with sometimes a heated soapstone or a hot, carpet-wrapped brick at our feet. We played pioneer—we were crouched in a covered wagon, and the amiable small-town sounds beyond, or the whistling wind of the open country were the threatening howls of wolves or Indians.

Even Santa Claus came by bobsled. A couple of weeks before Christmas his impending arrival was proclaimed by the businessmen. Everybody gathered downtown, kids shoving and falling off the curbs in frantic anticipation. Then came the sweet, familiar jangling of his sleighbells, and there was the old boy himself, waving a mittened paw and tossing out bags of candy while some assistant drove the team.

A free show at the movies followed. "To get us kids out of the way so our folks can buy our presents," smart-alecky older ones claimed. We were doubtful and stricken. But we'd just *seen* him.

"Aaah, that was just ole Matt McDermott dressed up," hooted the heretics sitting behind. And they jiggled the musty velour seat. "We peeked through the courthouse window and seen him stuffing a pillow down his pants!" It was too funny, and too awful to believe. Yet it didn't really matter. Sucking blissfully on the hard, painted candies, watching Tom Mix or Harold Lloyd, we were content in the awareness of some loving adult conspiracy on our behalf.

The fantasy of Santa Claus seemed not in the least at odds with the mail-order catalogs, over which we crouched, making long, drunken lists which must be whittled down to plausible proportions. Nor with the noisy bedlam of shopping in our little stores. Nor with the hum of Mama's sewing machine at night. Over and over we'd ask, "What for?" if only to hear the beloved reply: "What fur? Cat fur to make kitten britches!" Pressed, she might admit that she was helping Santa's elves. "He's not going to be able to do as much as he'd like to this year." Then, among the few new toys of Christmas morning we would find bean bags, doll clothes, little cloth purses for Sunday School.

The old pine chest in the store-room held all sorts of oddments from which she drew: Scraps of flannel left over from diapers, velvet and gingham, quilt blocks, buttons, embroidery cotton. Here she hid both her handiwork and her purchases; and it was understood by all that no one looked in the box. The most miserable Christmas I ever had was the year I yielded to temptation and found what I most desperately wanted, a real, working Ouija board.

Mother exchanged gifts with a number of chums who lived elsewhere—Aunt Tressa, Aunt Anna, Aunt Mabel, as we called them. She worked openly on their presents, tatting or crocheting doilies and edgings, her shuttle dipping like a little fat bird, the dainty beak of her crochet hook plucking and pulling and picking—almost tasting the threads. She wrapped her efforts in white tissue paper, thin as new snow, and bound them with silver cords. And those rectangles of white and silver seemed in their loveliness to be jeweled blocks for the palace of the Ice Princess.

By now she would have brought forth the family decorations— rough ropes of red and green to loop above the lace curtains and garland the living room. And several paper bells which lay flat until unfolded, when lo! they bloomed fat and full to hang in doorways and dance in the heat of the hardcoal stove. For us, as for most people, this was all. And while the churches boasted Christmas trees, they were almost unknown in private homes when I was very small.

I shall never forget our first one. Two gentle maiden ladies who lived next door called Mother over one day: and when she returned home she was excitedly bearing an enormous box. Desperate for its secret, we plagued her until she yielded at least initials: C. T. D. We spent almost as much time trying to guess their meaning as learning our pieces for the Christmas Eve program at the church.

This program, at first mostly songs and recitations, later a pageant, was as much a part of Christmas as hanging up our stockings. We practiced religiously, and if possible got a new dress. Snow squeaked underfoot and sparkled under the streetlights as the family walked to the church. Grandpa Griffith, who was janitor, always built a big fire early. The church was warm and spicy with the scent of the tall fir tree beside the stage. Standing over the hot-air register, we admired the way our skirts ballooned.

It seemed an unusually joyful program, even if Santa Claus did knock over the red cardboard fireplace, climbing out. Going home, we kicked up little skirls of snow, and flung ourselves down in it to fashion "angels" with our arms. We picked out the shepherd's star. Then, at Papa's annual announcement that he'd just spied reindeer over a roof just up the block, we scurried for bed. Where we lay hugging ourselves and listening to the sweet lullabye of Christmas Eve—parental voices murmuring, the rattle of paper, the tinkle and squeak of treasures unguessed.

Awake before daylight, we found Mama already in the room to restrain us. "Wait!" she said. Something strange was going on. Then when Papa called, "Ready, Rose," she led us forth—into fairyland. Or so it seemed. For there in the living room bloomed a miracle: a Christmas tree! Its candles twinkled and fluttered as if hosts of butterflies and birds had alighted on its branches. From its arms gleamed dozens of fragile beads and baubles and ornaments. We stared at it, eyes shining, too dazzled to speak.

And now we knew the secret of the box. C. T. D. "Christmas Tree Decorations," Mama laughed. "The Misses Spicer had them as young ladies in Europe and want our family to have them now."

This lovely gift became the basis for all the trees that followed. We augmented it with strings of popcorn, paper chains, gilded walnuts, and later, when they were plentiful, cranberries. The exquisite fragrance (and hazard) of the tallow candles was replaced by electric bulbs, while tinsel and icicles and fine new ornaments almost crowded out those exquisite early ones. But no tree, however splendid, will be as beautiful as that first one. And no gifts, however expensive or plentiful, can surpass the joy of those precious few we found under it that day.

*Today's Health* 1967

* * * F. Scott Fitzgerald

# My Middle West

 NE OF my most vivid memories is of coming back West from prep school and later from college at Christmas time. Those who went farther than Chicago would gather in the old dim Union Station at six o'clock of a December evening, with a few Chicago friends, already caught up in their own holiday gayeties, to bid them a hasty good-by. I remember the fur coats of the girls returning from Miss This-or-That's and the chatter of frozen breath and the hands waving overhead as we caught sight of old acquaintances, and the matching of invitations: "Are you going to the Ordways'? the Herseys'? the Schultzes'?" and the long green tickets clasped tight in our gloved hands. And last the murky yellow cars of the Chicago, Milwaukee and St. Paul railroad looking cheerful as Christmas itself on the tracks beside the gate.

When we pulled out into the winter night and the real snow, our snow, began to stretch out beside us and twinkle against the windows, and the dim lights of small Wisconsin stations moved by, a sharp wild brace came suddenly into the air. We drew in deep breaths of it as we walked back from dinner through the cold vestibules, unutterably aware of our identity with this country for one strange hour, before we melted indistinguishably into it again.

That's my Middle West—not the wheat or the prairies or the lost Swede towns, but the thrilling returning trains of my youth, and the street lamps and sleigh bells in the frosty dark and the shadows of holly wreaths thrown by lighted windows on the snow. I am part of that, a little solemn with the feel of those long winters. . . .

* * * May Traller

# Grandma's House Held Christmas in its Heart

 HRISTMAS was coming! You would know it by the way the blue-black clouds swung low over Half Moon Hill. You could tell it when you heard the red-bird shouting through the crisp air in the mornings.

And when you looked there he was, a scarlet splash against the dark glistening cedar boughs. But most of all we knew Christmas was coming by the buoyant feeling, the thrill which came to our hearts as we raced home from school on the last Friday before vacation for the Yuletide.

There had been a wonderful Christmas program and a tree at school, and I hugged to my heart the little blue glass hen which had been placed under the tree for me by the one who drew my name. We always drew names at school when Christmas time came.

We paused as usual on top of Half Moon Hill under the whispering pines and looked out across the illimitable expanse of undulating hills hung with eternal haze, blue as mystery. The hills, the pines, the heavens were singing and chanting, "Christmas is coming, Christmas is coming!"

The very clouds caught the lilt of it and echoed it in whispering snowflakes that tentatively wandered through the chill air.

"Do you think Santa Claus will know we will be at Grandma's on Christmas eve?" I asked anxiously, and the others answered convincingly, "Of co-o-oourse! Doesn't Santa Claus know everything?"

And above our heads the pines echoed sibilantly, "Yes-s-s-s, yes-s-s-s." Oh, the glorious wonder of approaching Christmas!

After an early noon meal on the day before Christmas we packed our boxes, baskets, bundles and food into the wagon—we always took the wagon when we drove to Grandma's—and started to the big house beyond Bittersweet Ridge.

Halfway through the singing woods we stopped. Dad got out and chopped down the fattest, merriest little tree we had ever seen and put it into the wagon. Christmas wouldn't be real without a tree from the singing woods.

And just as we started out again, Old Trim came loping after us with his funny catercornered gallop.

"Let him come," said Dad. "It would be a shame for even a dog to spend Christmas alone."

The smoke from Grandma's house was building a column from the chimney up to heaven when we caught sight of it. The house at the foot of the slope looked happy, and even before we reached the front door we could smell the mince pies baking and knew that the turkey already was hanging to freeze in the locust tree at the back kitchen door. Grandma would have cold biscuits saved for the stuffing.

As we went into the living room, the firelight burst into rosy bloom that sent the shadows scurrying under the sofa and the big old walnut chairs that stood about the room.

Some houses are made for music and dancing. Others are built to hold life and love and mystery. Grandma's house was made for the purpose of holding Christmas in its heart forever.

You could catch the echo of Christmas carols from attic to cellar, and the fringe of icicles along the branches of the cedars just outside jingled like Christmas chime bells every time a wind danced by. The old house simply shouted of yuletide from rafter to corners.

When the little tree had been set in the corner we hung it with sycamore balls wrapped in tinfoil, and no silver bubbles anywhere could have shone and danced more merrily among the dark green. There were ropes of bittersweet berries and popcorn, and Grandma had made molasses popcorn balls. We hung them here and there in the tree and couldn't help starting a circling dance about it singing,

Ho, ho, ho, who wouldn't go,
Ho, ho, ho, who wouldn't go,
Up on the housetop click, click, click,
Down through the chimney with good Saint Nick.

But with such glory as the little tree standing there waiting for the visit of that very saint of Christmas, we couldn't be noisy long.

Soon we snuggled down. The fire snapped saucy fingers, the cedars brushed the windows, and the wind in the chimney hummed a Christmas anthem. I glanced up to where my stocking hung from the mantle, drowsiness swept over me, and I dreamed of Santa Claus.

—*The Des Moines Register*, 1944

From "The Amanas Yesterday"          Photography by Dr. Christian Herrmann

* * * Grace Noll Crowell

# Let Us Keep Christmas

Whatever else be lost among the years,
Let us keep Christmas still a shining thing;
Whatever doubts assail us, or what fears,
Let us hold close one day, remembering
Its poignant meaning for the hearts of men.
Let us get back our childlike faith again.

Wealth may have taken wings, yet still there are
Clear windowpanes to glow with candlelight;
There are boughs for garlands, and a tinsel star
To tip some little fir tree's lifted height.
There is no heart too heavy or too sad,
But some small gift of love can make it glad.

And there are home-sweet rooms where laughter rings,
And we can sing the carols as of old.
Above the eastern hills a white star swings;
There is an ancient story to be told;
There are kind words and cheering words to say.
Let us be happy on the Christ Child's day.

* * * Clarence A. Andrews

# The Tall Ships of Christmas

 HE FIRST Christmas tree came to England in 1841, a gift from the German Prince Consort, Albert, to his wife, Queen Victoria. In no time at all, the custom of a decorated evergreen tree in churches and homes at Christmas time spread across the United States. The demand was greater than local woodlands could satisfy, and soon the vast, dark forests of northern Wisconsin and Minnesota and the Michigan peninsulas were providing the Christmas trees for the midwest.

These trees were only part of the rich harvest of lumber from these forests. The framing lumber and the shingles, the planks for walls and floors and doors, the boards for windows and cabinets, were shipped down the Wisconsin and Mississippi Rivers and down the Great Lakes in rafts or on tall-masted sailing schooners. The Mississippi River cities, Great Lakes cities in Michigan and Wisconsin, and Chicago were the funnels through which this lumber became the homes and shops for the ever-growing midwestern population.

To Chicagoans in particular, the lumber schooners on the Chicago River were so numerous that no one paid them any attention except for the times when it was necessary to open the wooden river bridges to let the ships pass. But on a dark November day in 1884 when the *Thal,* a squat schooner with two tall pine masts, was towed up the river and tied to a dock at Clark Street, passersby over the nearby bridge stopped and stared down at the ship, mouths agape. Piled high on its deck, from bow to stern, were hundreds of Christmas trees of all sizes and shapes. Even as they watched, a boy began tacking up a canvas sign:

THE CHRISTMAS-TREE SHIP    MY PRICES ARE THE LOWEST

Herman Schuenemann

The news raced through the city. Soon, newspaper reporters, sensing a story, were on board the *Thal,* asking for *Mr.* Schuenemann. They discovered the story was even better than they had thought; Herman Schuenemann, the boy who had put up the sign, a thirteen-year-old orphan from Wisconsin who lived with an elder brother, had conceived the idea of the Christmas Tree Ship, rented a relative's lumber schooner, hired its crew, and brought the vessel with its green cargo down from the snowbound Michigan peninsula.

By Christmas, this cargo of what was becoming Christmas's second great symbol was sold. The novelty of the venture and young Schuenemann's modest prices—small trees sold for as little as ten cents, six- to seven-footers for only a dollar—had captivated Chicagoans who had always bought their trees in vacant lots or from peddlers' wagons.

"I'll be back next year," Herman told his customers.

The following year Herman again sold all his trees, long before the dealers around the corner on South Water Street—Chicago's old downtown market place—had sold theirs.

The Christmas Tree Ship became a Chicago institution, and soon, its arrivals marked the symbolic beginning of the Christmas Season for many Chicago families. As the years passed, every November the *Thal* with its green cargo tied up at its berth on the south bank of the river at Clark Street. Children who had once visited the ship with their parents became adults and began bringing their own children to the ship.

Herman's success led other lumber schooner owners to try their luck. One of them, a Captain Clark of the *Kate Hinchman,* would borrow a buggy in Sturgeon Bay, Wisconsin and drive around the countryside, hiring youngsters to cut trees for him; he paid them as much as four dollars a day. "Smell 'em," Clark would tell potential Chicago buyers. "Don't that spicy smell remind you of the old piny woods down east? I never got together a cargo that gave me half the pleasure that I've got out of this one."

Pleasure such voyages might have been, but they had their perils. Herman's brother, Captain August Schuenemann, sank with the *Thal* in an 1898 Lake Michigan storm, and Herman transferred his business to the *Rouse Simmons,* a forty-four-year-old sailing ship.

The year before, Herman's customers had had the pleasure of meeting a young woman whose "sparkling eyes and ruddy cheeks were a delicate accompaniment to the pealing laughter and arched chest with which Captain

Herman announced his marriage."

"This is my wife Barbara," he said with pride and happiness.

That year many of Herman's customers returned with gifts for his bride. Others who saw the wedding announcement in Chicago's newspapers brought gifts with them. Herman had become more than an institution; he had become an honorary member of his customers' families.

Babies followed, The first was Elsie, who quickly became known as "the Christmas Tree girl." Twins, Pearl and Hazel, followed in 1900. These arrivals and other Schuenemann family news were duly reported in ever-lengthening newspapers stories about the family and its ship, attesting to the growing hold the family's story had taken on Chicago's heart.

Then tragedy struck the Schuenemann family again. On November 23, 1912, in a terrible storm, the *Rouse Simmons* with Herman, its crew of eighteen and all its trees, went down off Two Rivers, Wisconsin, two hundred miles north of its safe harbor at Clark Street.

The entire midwest was appalled by this tragedy. "Ships were taken off their regular runs, yachts raised their anchors and sailed out into the turbulent lake, and the Federal government was persuaded to lend its revenue cutters to join in the search. For a week they combed the combers in vain." Some say no trace of the ship was ever found; others report that "for years afterward fishermen pulled up traces of Herman's last load."

When reporters went to the Schuenemann home on North Clark Street, Barbara Schuenemann met them with a smile.

"Thank Chicago for its offer to help," she said. "But tell them we are not in need. Our home is paid for; there'll be a few dollars left over after the debts are paid; and I have my health. We will be all right. The captain would not wish me to take charity, no matter how kindly the donors."

"What will you do later?" she was asked. "Chicago wants to know your plans."

"What will I do?" she echoed. "Why, I shall get another ship and bring the children their Christmas trees — just as the captain would wish me to."

In 1913, Barbara Schuenemann shipped the usual 20,000 trees from Manistique in Michigan's Upper Peninsula by rail, and sold them in a North Clark Street store as near as the bridge as she could get. In 1914, she chartered the *Fearless,* and with Elsie and a crew of ten, went up to the snowpacked northern forests for trees.

From that time on until her death, Barbara Schuenemann, now known as "the Christmas Tree Lady," and Elsie never missed a year with their Christmas trees and greenery, although in later years she was often forced to ship by rail because she could not find a boat or assemble a crew.

In 1915, one of Chicago's greatest tragedies struck the site where the Schuenemanns sold their trees. On July 24, 1915, the excursion steamer *Eastland,* anchored in their spot, capsized as it was about to take more than 2,000 excursionists on a lake cruise; 812 men, women and children died in a few moments, even though more than half the ship was above water.

By Christmas of that year, Barbara and Elsie were virtually alone on the river with their trees. Rail rates were becoming cheaper and the once vast evergreen forests of the north were virtually depleted. Chicagoans were turning to trees brought in by train from the American South and West. Moreover, there was a growing sentiment that the Christmas tree itself was a waste of natural resources. Many midwesterners consequently refused to have a Christmas tree in their home.

By the end of World War I, the Schuenemann's first youthful customers were grey-haired but still they came back. Barbara Schuenemann was older too, her palms calloused from years of handling trees, her face wrinkled from tramping through the ever-diminishing forests in search of trees while icy winds slashed at her skin.

"I'm getting old and tired," Barbara told a friend at Christmas of 1923. "We haven't very much. But nobody gave me a penny and we owe no one. Elsie and the twins got better educations than their father or I ever had. The captain would have liked that. As long as my strength lasts, I shall bring the Christmas Tree Ship to Chicago every year. After me, maybe my daughters, or their children, when they are grown, will do the same. The captain would have wished it."

Barbara Schuenemann kept up the family Christmas Tree tradition until Christmas of 1932, even though in those last years she had to bring in all her trees by train. She died in 1933 in that first year of the Chicago Century of Progress.

The tradition of the Tall Ships that once brought Christmas trees is long gone now. Sadly, perhaps, the only monument to that era stands in Chicago's Irving Park Cemetery. There among the other headstones is one that bears the names of Herman and Barbara Schuenemann. Engraved also with a Christmas tree, it's a reminder of those romantic days when ships loaded to the deck with Christmas trees docked at the Clark Street bridge and heralded the start of the Christmas season.

* * * Terry Andrews

# Blue Christmas

HIS IS A STORY about Christmas, and about a box under our Christmas tree one year that wasn't big enough, by a long shot, to hold a bicycle. That box, brightly wrapped in blue tissue with a tag "Merry Christmas, Terry—love, Mom and Dad," was the object of my considerable attention, because I knew it held my main gift, and what I really wanted was a bicycle. And not any bicycle, but a particular blue bicycle from Johnston's Hardware Store on the Hill.

On the other side of the tree was another box, wrapped in red, with a tag "Merry Christmas, Steve—love, Mom and Dad." Steve, my nine-year-old brother, wanted an electric train, and he was sure that was what his package held.

It was 1958, my eleventh year, and we were living in Cedar Falls, a town I never really got to know because we moved from there to Iowa City the next fall.

We had a low, ranch-style house, pale green and brand new. It was a new street and a new neighborhood, dotted with expensive new homes.

The Hill was six blocks away and important to us, not only for its small shopping district but also because it was the site of the college my sister, Linda, 17, would attend next fall.

The Monday before Christmas, Steve and I headed for the Hill to do our Christmas shopping. Shivering, I plunged my hands as far into my pockets as they would go. The sky was ominously grey, and the cold wind which shook the bare branches of the trees overhead, seemed to cut right through my jacket.

"C'mon, Steve," I called impatiently to my brother, who had stopped to retrieve a can he was kicking along the sidewalk. "We'll never get there if we don't hurry."

He gave the can a big kick and ran by me as the can clinked off into the street. "Race ya," he cried.

We were off. I was a faster runner than he was, but sometimes with a head start he could beat me. I sprinted behind him, straining to catch up. He stopped at the corner, winded, his face red. "I won," he panted triumphantly.

Any other day I would have called him a cheater. But today was special, so I let him stay the victor. The Hill was in sight. Its lampposts were gaily strung with green cellophane chain and huge plastic candy canes that looked good enough to eat. Steve and I trudged up the hill that gave the small shopping area its name, past the soda shop where we sometimes got ice cream in the summer, past the pet store where we usually admired the parakeets and turtles. We were going to the five-and-dime to do our Christmas shopping—for the first time alone.

My brother had his savings from his piggy-bank clutched in his hand, and I had four dollars, some of which I'd earned raking the neighbor's yard, in my pocket.

At the dime store we paused long enough to look in the window. There were a host of wonderful things there—chocolate Santas, dolls with long hair, miniature bright red fire trucks with a hose that sprayed water.

"You could get that for me," I announced to my brother, pointing to a round blue sliding saucer which sat on a mound of artificial snow. "I'll share it with you."

"I only have sixty-five cents," he reminded me.

Then in we went, into the warm wonderful interior which smelled of candy and perfume and scented soap. We could have spent hours there, inspecting our way down each aisle, trying on sunglasses, fingering the sheer pastel scarves, eyeing the soda fountain.

Steve stopped by a jar of colored combs and carefully examined one. Then he looked at me. "Don't you have shopping to do?" he demanded.

I headed for the aisle that held envelopes, notebooks and stationery. My sister would need stationery to write to us, I thought. It was a perfect gift. I debated about buying my father a notebook, since he would be going back to college in Iowa City. (At 45!) Too ordinary, I thought. I wanted to give him something special, not something silly, like the green beanie his friends were planning!

My brother came around the corner and began looking at the pencils. I picked up the stationery I'd chosen and headed for the cash register in front. I had made my mother a set of hot pads, but I wanted to give her something else as well. Suddenly I spotted the perfect gift, a pair of pale blue earrings that would just match her new dress.

I had enough money left to buy baseball cards, bubble gum and a miniature flashlight for Steve. After I paid for my presents I waited for him outside, tactfully, so I wouldn't see what he'd gotten me.

Soon he emerged, beaming, a small bag in one hand, a nickel in the other. "Let's go wrap them," he said.

We went home by way of the hardware store, so I could look at my bike. It wasn't my bike actually, but I was saving money to buy it. I wanted it more than anything else in the world. It was a slim blue Italian model — blue was my favorite color that year — and I'd never seen another one like it. I planned to ride it to school, to the ice cream shop, and to see my best friend Cathy, even though she only lived a half block away from me. Next fall, I'd ride it all over Iowa City.

The hardware store was busy, and Mr. Johnston was waiting on a customer. He wouldn't have time to talk today. I would take a quick look at my bike and be on my way. My brother waited by the sporting goods while I went to the back where the bicycles were. There it was, on the end, as blue as the whole sky, just waiting to be ridden. I reached over to touch the blue and white seat, and stopped cold. Hanging from the handlebar was a tag, handwritten in capital letters. SOLD, it said.

It seemed like my heart stopped and time stood still. For three months, ever since the first day I saw it, I'd been saving my money to buy that blue bike.

I ran from the store, fighting back tears. Now somebody else would ride down College Street on my bike, somebody I knew, or, worse yet, a stranger who would carelessly leave it out in the rain and snow to rust and grow old.

On the way home, Steve and I walked slowly. I didn't notice the cold. He wanted to talk, but I was thinking about the bicycle that almost was, the bicycle that wouldn't be. One thing was certain. I could break open my bank. I no longer needed the twelve dollars I'd saved. I started to think of what I would buy with it.

This, our last Christmas in Cedar Falls, would be a truly blue

Christmas now, I knew. Next year, we would no longer have the ranch house with its two fireplaces. Instead, we would have a tiny tin barracks left over from World War II, so small it was barely larger than my bedroom in Cedar Falls. Instead of a fireplace it would have an oilstove; instead of a picture window looking out over a spacious green lawn, it would have windows so high you couldn't see out and no lawn at all. My mother said we had to save money, and cut back. She was going to find a job while my father went to school. There'd be no money for a blue bicycle then.

I didn't look forward to the prospect of cutting back or moving. I liked Cedar Falls, the shops on the Hill, my school, and my best friend Cathy. But I knew education was important. It had brought us to the new ranch-style with the huge sloping lawn planted with Russian olive trees and weeping willows. That house was miles and miles from the ramshackle houses my father had grown up in, dark, drafty tinderboxes bordering smelly, smoky factories. And it would take us even further — to the university town where my father hoped to get a Ph.D. degree, and then to some other university town where he would become a professor.

If I had my blue bike, I thought brightly, I wouldn't mind moving so much. Then, remembering how much my father had gone without as a boy, I decided to put the bicycle out of my mind. There was Christmas to think about, and presents to wrap.

By the time my brother and I got home, my spirits had picked up and we burst excitedly through the door, throwing off our jackets and hats. I heard Bing Crosby on the record player singing "White Christmas." That meant my father had gotten out his Christmas records while we were gone. He was sitting by the fireplace, where a fire was crackling reading. Occasionally he'd sing a few bars, his off key tenor voice echoing Crosby's.

My mother was baking, humming as she worked. She was making sugar cookies shaped like bells and reindeer, sprinkled with red and green sugar. My brother and I sat down and had two each, warm from the oven, at the picnic table we ate from in our kitchen. Next she would make date pinwheels, little circles of dough and date filling that melted in my mouth. The tempting scent of cookies baking drifted through the warm and cozy house from room to room, as Bing Crosby sang and I wrapped my packages. When I put them under the tree I spotted several small rectangular packages that my brother had wrapped.

One was addressed to me. "Merry Christmas, Terry," the card read, "and no peeking."

A piece of tinsel had fallen off the tree and I put it back on a low branch, then stepped back to admire the tree. Decorating it was a family affair, and each year we dragged out the box of ornaments and happily examined its contents. There were little candle-shaped lights with colored water inside that bubbled when you plugged them in. There was tinsel, which we carefully removed from the tree each year and saved. There were fragile glass balls that caught the light in little rainbows, paper chains, and popcorn we strung with a needle.

At night, when the room was dark and the Christmas tree lights were on, the living room seemed to take on a special glow, a blue glow, as if that tree were the center of the universe and all the promise of the world lay in that room. That tree represented warmth, happiness security. It made me feel good the way my favorite poem made me feel good, that Robert Frost poem that I found in one of my father's books. It began "Whose woods these are I think I know," a poem about watching the woods fill up with snow, about solitude, about responsibility, but most of all, about catching, for a moment, a glimpse of peace.

"Look," my mother said, "it's snowing."

The sky that had threatened snow all day opened up, and soft flakes fell softly to the ground, piling up around the steps, blanketing the yard, and draping the small pine trees outside. A hush came over the neighborhood and in every picture window, it seemed, the colored lights of Christmas trees twinkled. Even the snow shimmered, catching and reflecting the blue lights strung on trees across the street.

After dinner my father told about Christmas when he was a boy. He told about the time there wasn't enough money for presents, or even food. The times he went hungry. The Christmases his father came home drunk. It was a faraway world that I only knew through his stories, and even though I had seen the rundown houses where he had grown up, I had trouble feeling the reality of going hungry, of going without presents on Christmas day.

Some of his Christmases were happy, and those were the ones I liked to hear about best. I liked to hear about the year he and his brother got a wooden sled, which they found leaning in the snow against their house on a bright Christmas morning. I liked to imagine my father going down hill at top speed, the snow flying in his face, momentarily blinding him, his peals of laughter.

But I would always think about going hungry. I secretly hoped I would never know a Christmas without date pinwheel cookies, and the oranges my mother always put in my stocking.

Suddenly I knew what I would give my father for Christmas — the money I saved for my bicycle. I ran to my room, and on a piece of paper I wrote 'Dear Dad, this is for your education.' I carefully folded the paper and in it I put the money I had saved for my bicycle — twelve one-dollar bills. I put the paper in a shoebox. He'd never guess in a million years what a shoebox as light as a feather held. Carefully I wrapped it and put it under the tree.

And then, it was Christmas! Christmas morning, and my brother and I were up at dawn, trying to rouse my parents from their bed. We waited impatiently while my mother made her way slowly to the kitchen and started the coffee in the percolator. My brother and I poked at the presents under the tree, and emptied our stockings of their ribbon candy, oranges, apples and trinkets. Couldn't my mother hurry? Why did they have to have coffee?

Finally the great moment came, as we all assembled around the tree. The anticipation was high. I had come to terms with the fact that there would be no bicycle, but that big box held something else, some wonderful surprise. I knew that. We began to open our presents. My grandmother had sent me pajamas. She had given my sister embroidered pillow cases. My sister had given my father a moustache cup for drinking his coffee. My brother opened a football, and whooped.

Then there was the big box for me, and I shook it to see if it rattled. It didn't.

"Try to guess," my mother said. I couldn't and finally ripped the paper from it. There inside was the big blue saucer from the five and dime. It had snowed just in time. My father opened a red flannel shirt my sister had made, and my mother opened the comb from my brother and ran it appreciatively through her hair. "You sweetheart," she said to Steve. My sister opened the stationery and laughed. "I guess this means I'll have to write," she said, giving me a hug.

Finally, my brother picked up his big box. He started to say "A saucer for —" and then something in the box rattled. His eyes opened wide. With my mother cautioning him to save the paper, he gently opened the box. It was an electric train set with a cattle car and a yellow caboose.

"It's just like the Illinois Central," he said.

Then I saw my father holding the shoebox, a puzzled gleam in his eyes. Carefully he untied the ribbon and undid the paper. He reached inside and slowly withdrew the note.

For once he didn't say anything. When he finished reading what I had written, he looked at me, then my mother. His eyes seemed to fill with tears.

Had I ruined Christmas? We all watched him in uneasy silence. Then, as he handed the note to my mother, he stood up, put on his new shirt, tucked his new comb in one pocket and the money in the other. "Looks like I'm all ready for college," he said, laughing.

Then his expression changed and he looked at all of us. "This is the most wonderful Christmas I've ever had. I hope it is for you too," he said. He winked at my mother.

My mother was smoothing the hot pads I had given her with her hands. She had put on the blue earrings. The way she smiled at me showed how pleased she was.

While my father was pretending to be drinking from his moustache cup. I picked up the coal black locomotive from my brother's train. "It's beautiful," I said.

He whispered, "Maybe you'll get a bike for your birthday."

"Maybe," I acknowledged. My birthday was eleven months off, and the coasting hills would have to do without me for now.

But then a realization came over me, suddenly, as I picked up the blue pencils my brother had given me. Christmas was more than giving presents, or receiving presents.

It was my brother stretching his allowance to buy us gifts. It was the care I had put into making those hot pads. It was my sister being there, before she went to college. It was my mother bustling in the kitchen, singing "Silent Night," and my father getting out his Bing Crosby record for the umpteenth time. It was carols and cookies and colored lights, a family in a small town on a morning when the snow fell thick and fast. It was love and sharing and being together. It was intangible stuff—memories, tradition, hope. It was catching, for a moment, a glimpse of peace.

My mother interrupted my thoughts. "Terry, could you please see if the coffee is ready?"

Dutifully I hurried off to the kitchen, where I could smell a cinnamon coffee cake baking. My mouth watered. "It's ready," I called, and I took out two coffee cups. Then I turned to see if the plates were on the table for breakfast.

I could not believe my eyes. There, parked next to the picnic table, was the bicycle from the hardware store, shinier, sleeker and bluer than it had ever been before, shimmering like a vision. Taking a deep breath, I ran over and touched the gleaming chrome, the leather seat, the tires.

Softly then Bing Crosby began singing "White Christmas" in the living room. I smiled. It might be a white Christmas for everyone else, with plump snow-capped evergreens on soft white lawns. It was a blue Christmas for me. Blue was the color of promise and possibility, of next year and always, of the roads I would follow, on that bike and others. Blue was the top of the hill, the wind at my back, freedom. With a flourish I kicked up the kickstand and wheeled my bike toward the front door.

*Messenger*
John Page, 1969

* * * Phil Stong

# Christmas in Iowa

ET'S GO HOME for Christmas." That is an airy phrase, a soap bubble of an idea that drifts into our minds in early December, more and more brightly lit, as we grow older, with memories of earlier Christmases, the old house, the folks, the home town.

The idea hits me almost every year, and I begin to pack for *my* home town, forgetting all over again that if there is one thing harder than to make strangers believe such a town as Keosauqua, Iowa, exists, it is to get there. Trains and planes and buses avoid it, and typical Corn Belt blizzards have a way of swooping down from the North Pole to glaze the roads between Keosauqua and the towns that do have such exotic forms of getting places.

There is no road, however, that my brother Jo can't negotiate, even though radios in neighboring states are blatting, "Where is the penicillin that left Fargo yesterday by bobsled?"

And where, oh where are the Stongs who set out so gaily on the Twentieth Century from New York? Well, I can tell you where they are for five hours of the trip—they are being batted around the Chicago railroad yards in that famous Pullman which is the answer to Mr. Robert Young's advertising campaign of several years ago: "A hog can cross the country without changing trains—but you can't." And what is happening to them shouldn't—and doesn't—happen to a hog, because a hog ping-ponged like that around Chicago for five hours would lose pounds of lard and the shipper would complain.

The Stongs, having shipped themselves, can't complain. They can just eat the limp sandwiches brought from New York—for the diner goes off early in the morning—and watch the black slush of the freight yards rolling now backward, now forward till, with a final vicious jerk, we are hooked onto the Chief and at last rolling home for Christmas.

The fat, flat farm lands of northwest Illinois with their groups of prosperous white buildings are the first glimpse of home. The place names, too, have the right sound: Galesburg of Abraham Lincoln, and the Spoon River of Edgar Lee Masters, Moline, where the plows come from. Then one more river to cross, the biggest of them all.

Clicking over the great bridge across the Mississippi, we can see the lights of Fort Madison, though we know the Chief will dump us in outer darkness, somewhere in the railroad yards with all our luggage. The Fort Madison station was not planned for long trains like this, which are hell-bent for Hollywood and not concerned with whether we break our necks over railroad tracks or get hit by a locomotive before my brother finds us with his flashlight.

He always finds us eventually, and we are off through forty miles of blizzard. But this is, after all, Christmas Eve, and we are almost home for Christmas. The town of Donnellson slips by, a speckle of lights veiled by falling snow, and then the bridge at Farmington. It is quite dark now, and getting colder.

"How are things?" I ask my brother Jo.

"Pretty good," he says. He knows exactly what I mean. Christmas in Iowa is the climax of the year, the time of summing up. "This storm is good for business." And I know what he means. Henry Strickling's drugstore and Priebe's department store and the electrical shops will get the last-minute shopping that might otherwise have gone to Ottumwa or even to Des Moines.

We have climbed the high hill above the Des Moines River, and there is my home town, a crescent of red and green and yellow lights spooning around the river bend, where, a hundred years ago, the little steamboats connecting the Mississippi with the center of Iowa would have been discharging passengers for the town's two oversize hotels—one gone now, gone with the boats.

But that's all right. We don't get so many strangers now—hardly any at Christmastime. Everybody in Keosauqua on Christmas Eve is home for Christmas, like us. It is cozy.

The town was brighter last Christmas Eve than I had ever seen it, with outdoor Christmas trees and house lights, partly, I must admit, because the civic clubs were holding a contest for the best holiday decorations. The prizes did not total a million dollars, but it takes only a five-dollar prize to make a Keosauquan put out six dollars in materials and twenty in effort to be in the running for any competition. We turned in at my mother's house, across the street from Jo's, and the colored electric candles sat in each window just as they sat that first winter after electricity came to town in 1903, and every year since. The distinctive smell of the house, clean, warm, welcoming, was the same too.

And there was mother, up to her ears in Christmas wrappings—she has always opened her packages the moment they came, in spite of the labels—and bright-eyed with excitement. Her main problem was oranges—the house was full of them, sent by crates and bushels from relatives and old friends, Iowans all, who in their later years go to Florida and California as inevitably as sparks fly upward.

"Of course," she says staunchly, "you *can't* have too many oranges."

"Maybe not," say I, remembering the days when an orange had just one use to fill the toe of a Christmas stocking; three boys in our family—three oranges a year. "And grapefruit? Do you remember the first ones we ever saw, in 1906? Dad brought them from Des Moines—a new fruit, said to be a cross between an orange and a lemon, which they aren't. We tasted them cautiously, and you said you *hoped* they weren't poison."

"I never did," says mother, lying in her teeth.

Jo and his wife Eleanore and Virginia and I spent a dissipated evening playing a quarrelsome card game called "Scram," unknown to us till that moment, which Virginia recognized as a variant of blackjack, with the result that she had piled up sixty cents in winnings before I recovered and reduced my losses to a quarter.

Mother said, "It seems like the old days when you were all running around and yelling at each other." Not so very much like the old days, I thought. Cards weren't respectable in Keosauqua when I was young.

Looking out the window at half past ten, I saw the outdoor Christmas trees flickering out, and the windows of the houses back of them. A few lamps will be stealthily turned on later, while presents are put around the indoor trees and stockings are stuffed. I'm convinced parents get more fun filling the stockings than children do emptying them.

Then, soon after midnight, the last lights go out.

Other times, other Christmas Eves. If this were December twenty-fourth, a few years before the First World War, I'd be lying, not on an innerspring mattress, but with my two cousins in a double bed at Linwood Farm, two miles from town—a bed so vast that we had to turn crossways to kick one another. It was one of those enormous black-walnut pieces—if the headboard had fallen on us we might not have been noticed among the sheets.

In this stronghold we whispered happily about the traps we had set for Santa Claus—one, a thread looped to John's toe, and another of my devising, a newspaper spread over the hearthstone on top of coarse cattle salt, guaranteed to crackle under his feet louder than that gaggle of geese that once saved Rome.

While vowing absolute wakefulness, we went to sleep.

Next morning there was no sign of the traps, not even the string on young John's toe. Santa Claus had outsmarted us. But I had other things on my mind, in particular my invaluable dollar watch with a solid gold chain—solid chain, anyway—and my silk handkerchief, violet, with embroidered fleurs-de-lis in the corners, with which I intended to overcome all the wonder girls in the second grade.

Dietetics was then unknown beyond "Lots of milk" and "A full stummick makes a full child." The Christmas dinner was prepared accordingly, Dickensian fashion. I can remember five or six Christmas dinners in the next few years, but I can't remember a thing after one o'clock till we piled in the buggy, went to sleep, and were shoved into our beds two miles away.

The ordinary Thanksgiving or Christmas dinner for a person of about my years and swallowing ability, in 1908, would have been:

  1 entire leg of a large turkey with some white meat
  1/2 pt. sage and onion dressing
  1 pt. mashed potatoes; gravy, with giblets fished for
  1/2 pt. mashed turnips
  1/3 large loaf bread; 8 oz. butter; jams, varied
  1 pt. cranberries, pickles, preserves, etc.
  1 pt. sundry vegetables; onions, beets, peas, limas, etc.
  1 pt. milk (Doesn't count—soaks in)

1 pt. sweet cider (Same)
1/4 mince pie
Oranges, celery, olives, candy, to fill
This is far beyond the capacity of the human (a vague term) stommick, of course, but it is well within the capacity of the entire boy. This estimate is not excessive; in fact, it is timorously conservative. About halfway through the meal Great-Aunt Beatie would tell us again of a little boy of her acquaintance who ate so much he busted his stummick and died in prolonged and horrible agonies. We never did learn whether he busted inside only or whether he spilled. But we felt nothing but contempt for the feeble wretch.

Just before I fell asleep on Christmas Eve in 1951, I thought about my father. If he were alive and running his general store—and not the post office, as he did in the last decade of his life—he would be still, at this late hour, running up and down the hill to open up again and again for some last-minute, desperate shopper. And tomorrow, while we all stuffed ourselves with turkey, he would be taking tea and toast for his invariable Christmas migraine. There are more kinds of service in a town like Keosauqua than R. H. Macy or Marshall Field or John Wanamaker ever dreamed of.

In the morning, after pancakes and country sausage and present-opening, I was encouraged by my wife and my mother to get the heck out of the way while they swept out the sea of Christmas wrappings and got back to basting the turkey.

From the front steps I could see a fine clear sweep of snow down to Main Street and a block beyond to the river. On a Flexible Flyer, now, I could make it in nothing flat, or even on that little old sled my father made me when I was three, out of a grocery box set on runners. A steering bar is not much use, anyway, at forty miles an hour, which was about the speed the younger generation was making at that moment, down the street.

Halfway down the hill I met one small boy who was not runnerborne this morning, Jimmy Worrell, the doctor's son. "Well, Jimmy," I said, "have a good Christmas?"

He looked at me glumly. "I've seen better." A pause. "Dad got himself an electric train—for me. I wanted a bike."

There was one other realist in town to match Jimmy. I heard about her a few minutes later, from Junior Nickelson, who was just coming out of his auto-supply-and-gadget store.

"How's business?" he answered me, waving at an almost empty display window. "Practically sold out, electric irons, fans, hairdryers, toasters—and trains. Say, has this town got trains! You hear about Bruce?" He was speaking of Bruce Barton, our Van Buren County Hospital superintendent. "Well, his wife came in and looked over all my toy trains and the fixin's—signal towers, depots, bridges. The Bartons haven't got any kids. So I asked her, 'How old is the little boy you're giving it to?' And she looked me right in the eye and said, 'The little boy is about forty.' She was just daring me to snicker."

Too bad Virginia isn't here, I thought. I've never had an electric train myself. In my day it was Erector sets mostly, and the towers I built with them always leaned farther than the one at Pisa, but I never intended to show up Galileo. I do have some toys at home, though, my microscope, my Army-surplus telescope, a thing that pushes out a cigarette, lights it and smokes it for me and stamps out the butt—but not one electric train.

Through the door of the drugstore I saw Henry Strickling, whose father established the store about half a century ago. Henry was tidying the few remaining Christmas cards on a counter, in a complacent way. "Hi," he said. "Just came down to look over the patent medicine shelf before the bellyaches begin. There'll some calls for them tonight, but nothing like we used to have. Dad used to sell about twenty kinds of stomach stuff, mixtures of red pepper, soda, senna, cascara, paregoric, bromides—most of them with a very good sound alcoholic base. Very comforting, if not curative.

"Sold three bottles of castor oil last night to the three worst pessimists in town. But mostly it was gift stuff—perfume and notepaper and candy and bath salts and sachet and toilet water—and more perfume. Anybody that goes to the movies in this town for the next few weeks is going to get asphyxiated with gardenia and lilac and Memory of Sin. Dad would be surprised at how his pharmacy has turned into a gol-darned general store."

He looked up at me gravely. "I was thinking last night about your father's store, wishing he was back in it."

"So was I," I said. "Guess I'll walk down past it now."

"Well," he said, shaking his head. Then he brightened. "You going out to Linwood today?"

I nodded. "We're all going out this afternoon."

"Good. That'll be nice for your mother. People don't congregate enough nowadays. Instead of fifteen, twenty at the table, ten makes a big crowd. Don't know where people have got to. The town had about fourteen hundred when you and I were kids, and it's got eleven hundred and four now—and several prospects I know of. Ought to be enough to fill a Christmas table."

He stood on his frosty doorstep waving at me as I turned down Main Street towards the site of B. J. STONG, VARIETY GOODS. Henry's kindly headshake wasn't really necessary. I was not going down to look at the old building, any more than I was really seeing the black-glass-and-chromium store fronts which are the outward and visible sign of farm prosperity in the 1940's. On the sidewalk in front of B. J. STONG, VARIETY GOODS, I looked—not at the neglected, dusty windows with sacks of chicken feed behind, but back through more than forty years, to a shadowy candy counter of 1908, officially out of bounds, but always somehow open—like everything my father had—to his three small boys. On the right wall I still saw the rows of shoe-boxes—the best work shoes St. Louis manufactured, $2.50 a pair, or to a customer who liked to bargain, $2.55, with a pair of socks thrown in.

Off a table there in the middle, my schoolbooks came, second or third or fourth hand from earlier generations of students who made the store a clearinghouse.

At the far back were the wallpaper racks, almost empty of wallpaper in the winter, but holding on Christmas Eve about 200 carefully labeled parcels, left till the last minute by the parents of 200 Junior G-men set on anticipating Santa Claus.

In the cubicle at the rear—lost in darkness now—my father kept his books, and *his* toys, the ones I sent him at Christmas after I grew up: a barometer that was consulted with a faith that passeth understanding by everyone in town who planned a picnic or a journey; a small radio; and a pocket watch with an alarm, which he dutifully set to remind himself of things, though the bell scared him silly every time it rang inside his pocket. "Every time the darn thing goes off I jump clear out of my chair."

As though that bell had rung again, I looked at my own watch. The turkey would be done, and if I didn't hurry home, "the skin would crackle off," a mishap that always upset mother. I trotted up the hill at a zigzag between sleds and unseasonal velocipedes and feet wobbling on new roller skates.

The skin had not crackled off, but before we finished, mine almost did. Not so Gargantuan as it used to be, the Iowa Christmas dinner is still a challenge to one who has been living in the effete East for twenty-seven years. One feudal touch, praise be, was missing. "What!" I said. "No peacock?"

Mother laughed. Back in the days when her sainted father was lord of Linwood Farm, he had, after reading *When Knighthood Was in Flower*, stocked the place with peafowl, which fought the hens, scared the horses, chased us children and rent the air with hideous complaint.

Everybody was heartily sick of them before long, except grandpa, a fairly determined character. But even determined characters, when they see peacocks chasing their hens, have been known to change their minds.

On the day before Christmas, 1908, coming out the kitchen door, I saw my baronial grandfather hopping mad. Squawking at him, with tail outspread, was the largest, maddest peacock of them all. Grandpa picked up a stick and threw it. Iowans are good pitchers—witness Bob Feller.

Next day the bird appeared, brown and bulging with sage stuffing on the Haviland platter, with two-foot, shimmering tail feathers set up at the appropriate end.

The gray goose of Southern folk song had nothing on that fowl. "The knife wouldn't cut 'im, the fawk wouldn't stick 'im," if we'd dared to "thro 'im in the hawg-pen," he'd have "broke the hawgs' teeth in." As it was, he just broke our teeth in, while everybody said how beautful his tail was. So little of him was eaten he may well have ended like the gray goose, "flyin' toward the ocean, with a long strang o'peachicks behind 'im."

Grandpa was not licked. Next Christmas we had another peacock. But we also had a turkey and a suckling pig and assorted roasts. By the year after that, the rest of the flock had disappeared, and no questions asked.

"Well," said mother obstinately on Christmas Day of 1951, "you were all very mean to papa. That peacock had a good flavor." How filial can you get?

Jo brought the car over to take us around town and out to Linwood. By rights, Lea Beggs, grandpa's hired man, ought to be out there at the curb with the surrey, waiting for us to tuck ourselves under the rainproof roof with our feet on carpet-covered hot bricks. But Jo's Packard is nice, too, and it can do a tour of the town before going two miles over the river and through the woods to Linwood.

I always like to drop in at the County Farm on Christmas to see my friends. Our County Farm is not a poorhouse, though it does have some residents who have no money. It also has a number of elderly persons, left alone and too old to run their farms, who have furnished their own rooms, made a reasonable deed to the county and moved in, knowing that for the rest of their lives they will lack for nothing—not even cribbage partners.

I was sad this Christmas that Steve was not there. My old friend Steve, the Greek popcorn seller, who, after being skinned of his last dollar and his popcorn stand by a couple of slick Illinois operators, quietly starved—almost, until the town found out about it and whisked him into a more comfortable home than he had ever known. For years I used to send Steve a hundred of the foulest cigars ever made—the brand he liked—and he sent me several pounds of hickory-nut meats, picked on the farm and shelled by his arthritic hands.

On only one other occasion did I ever hear of people being hungry in Keosauqua—a Christmas Eve when the father of a new family in town bought only corn meal at the grocery. The grocer was curious. "What are you doing with that stuff for Christmas?"

"Makin' fried mush. I got a side of bacon—partly."

"Gosh Almighty," said the grocer, and began to toss real food into a basket. "It's tough getting to town too late to raise anything but winter wheat. Next year it'll be better."

The word spread around town—fried mush on Christmas—in *Keosauqua*! The newcomers would probably have spent an easier Christmas with the sowbelly and mush than they did with the tide of visitors who poured in the next day, bringing turkey and hams and pies and dolls and Teddy bears.

Back from the County Farm, Jo turned up Courthouse Hill. The courthouse, the oldest, now, in Iowa, is of honest native limestone and brick, painted a dishonest, gloomy brown—a tall dour building looming over the lighted Christmas tree in front (Abe Lincoln and Bob Ingersoll had clients here). The small jail nearby is cozier. It is oftener empty than full, and when it isn't, it is full of a drunken driver or two—Keosauqua is tough about them, with two main highways through town—or perhaps full of somebody who has tried to sock somebody else in an argument over politics. We rode by, with the comfortable knowledge that if there was anybody in jail, he was having turkey too—with cranberry sauce.

The Van Buren County Hospital is a streamlined, modern mirage in the Keosauqua landscape, still a surprise to old-timers like me, but to the town a triumph and an Ark. Since the hospital came three years ago, five doctors have come to town. Before that, serious sickness meant an ambulance ride of eighteen miles to Fairfield, and sometimes you were Dead on Arrival. Jo turned in at the hospital to give us a glimpse of the handsome lobby. Supt. Bruce Barton was not around. "Probably at home playing with his train," said Jo.

We drove up the Long Lane and over the Des Moines River by the Pittsburg Bridge, crossed Chequest Creek by a smaller one, and ran along the river front of Linwood. It looks about as it always has, since Grandpa Duffield came home from the Gold Rush in 1852 with enough money to buy the land and build the house of bricks from his own clay fired in his own kiln. As we turned from the river road up the long approach to the house, I was glad I, too, had dug some gold in California twenty years ago, enough to buy this old place back into the family. My digging was done in a movie studio, but it was just as strenuous as grandpa's.

The lighted house looked as it always had, warm and welcoming in the Christmas dusk. The Church Tree, where the first settlers held their services before they had a church building, is a gaunt old dying giant now.

This rock-top driveway is different from the old one—up which grandpa used to urge the horses through heavy mud with Methodist curses—"By George!" "By Jocks!" "Confound it!"

He would be surprised to know that under that "tarnation" useless rocky patch on our Ralston Branch place lay all this fine limestone, which, crushed, has surfaced many of the county roads in addition to this driveway.

He would be surprised, too, at the new well, the water pipe to the barns, and at other changes inside the house. My partner-tenant, Cecil Ridgeway, and Mrs. Ridgeway and the young Ridgeways were grouped in the doorway, and before the "Merry Christmases" were finished, Mrs. Cecil was drawing Virginia and mother away to look at her electric kitchen and the shiny bathroom, new since rural electrification finally arrived in this section the year before.

Jo and I stayed in the kitchen with Cecil and the kids, every one of them a good farmer except, perhaps, the baby, and even he had loaned his nursing bottles to the weak new-born lambs that Mrs. Cecil brings into the kitchen every spring.

Grandpa would have liked those children, maybe better than he liked us. For my cousins and brothers and I were farmers only under protest, especially I.

"Well, Cecil," I said, somewhat timidly, "how are things?" I glanced at his right arm. I had not seen him since he had caught it in a hay baler and had won a long fight against amputation, while farming nearly five hundred acres of vigorous, demanding Iowa soil.

"Fine," he said. "The barns are full and we're going to have a big crop of sheep and hogs and cattle, come spring." He glanced down at his arm too. "I'm getting fair use of it—and my left arm's mighty good."

As gallant a remark as one now a part of legend in Keosauqua—the answer made by Thad Sherod when, just after his restaurant burned down without insurance, someone asked him with clumsy sympathy, "How are things?"

"O.K.," said Thad. "I had a good breakfast, and it ain't time for dinner yet."

"It's time for supper," said mother, coming back from the front parlor, which she always likes to visit when she is at Linwood because my father courted her there. "I've been standing in the bay window looking at the river and thinking—it hasn't changed, though everything else has."

"But it has changed," I said. "It's added twenty-two acres to this farm since I owned it."

"That isn't what I meant," said mother, and of course it wasn't.

Mrs. Ridgeway wanted us to stay and eat with them, but mother said, "I've got half a turkey at home, and when the children go back East, what will I do with it?"

So we got into the car and drove down toward the changing, unchanging river. There were no sleighs on the ice tonight, but our sleigh was safe back there in the carriage house, where it has always been since 1890. And the same stars were coming out over my home town.

*Holiday*, 1951

113

* * * [Charles] Badger Clark (1883-1957)

# The Christmas Trail

HE WIND is blowin' cold down the mountain tips
   of snow
And cross the ranges layin' brown and dead;
It's cryin' through the valley trees that wear the
   mistletoe
And mournin' with the gray clouds overhead.
   Yet it's sweet with the beat of my little hawses's feet
And I whistle like the air was warm and blue;
For I'm ridin' up the Christmas trail to you,
      Old Folks,
I'm a-ridin' up the Christmas trail to you.

The coyote's winter howl cuts the dusk behind the hill,
But the ranch's shinin' window I kin see;
And though I don't deserve it, and I reckon never will,
There'll be room beside the fire kep' for me.
Skimp my plate 'cause I'm late. Let me hit the old kid gait,
For tonight I'm stumblin' tired of the new.
And I'm ridin' up the Christmas trail to you,
      Old Folks,
I'm a-ridin' up the Christmas trail to you.

From *Sun and Saddle Leather*
1915

* * * Hartzell Spence

# Christmas in the Parsonage

 HRISTMAS ALWAYS was an exciting Holiday. The family was a unit as at no other time, and father, who throughout the year had been big brother and uncle to the entire community, was remembered by scores of parishioners as though he belonged to their own households.

One of our greatest Christmases occurred at Fort Dodge. It was the last of the old-fashioned yuletide festivals, for war had come before the winter of 1914, and after the war Christmas was not the same.

In 1913 the merchant had not yet become the beneficiary; Christ in the manger was still worshipped. Most of the people of Fort Dodge made their own gifts, supplementing them by such items as sleds and skates, which they could not handily produce at home. The parsonage celebration began two weeks earlier than that of our neighbors because of the ceremony of packing a box for our Canadian relatives. A week's lull followed, until a box arrived from Canada, after which we turned to preparations for the church Christmas; we were not permitted to forget that first place was reserved for the Christ child, whose birthday the holy day was. We children learned verses and attended rehearsals for the Christmas pageant. A few days before Christmas a committee appeared at the parsonage with tubs of candy and nuts and packed sacks for Santa Claus to give every member of the Sunday School on Christmas Eve. We loved this, because any candy left over was ours.

Then downtown on the day before Christmas went the whole family to select the Christmas tree. Father examined it for durability, mother for size, we children for symmetry. We went to Woolworth's to augment the ornaments saved from year to year. Eileen, Fraser, and I would have run riot here had not father and mother patiently curbed our extravagance both in money and taste. If mother shook her head, we rejected a gaudy ornament in favor of one more conventional; if father frowned, we were overreaching the budget.

Home again with our booty, we shared the intoxicating excitement of dressing the tree, which father enjoyed to the extent of writing his sermon on a clip board in the living room instead of in his study. When the ornaments were in place, we opened the big bundle from the Canadian relatives and hefted, rattled, and sniffed the individual packets for possible identification, father as curious as the rest of us. At the same time we helped father and mother to sort packages from other towns where father had served as pastor, and we arranged the offerings from his parishioners in Fort Dodge.

In the evening we went to the church and after the Christmas Eve service hurried home to appear in the window when the choir came by to sing carols. We smiled and beamed our appreciation, and then Eileen and I went outside to join the carolers on their round of the hospitals, the jail, and the homes of shut-in church members. This lasted until ten o'clock, or later if falling snow enhanced the festivities.

Christmas morning we were up early. Church members began to call at seven o'clock and continued to drop in throughout the day, bringing gifts and messages. There were a few presents we could count on: the Mohnike girls' homemade candy, Tony Roffel's cut glass or Haviland, Mr. McCutcheon's barrel of apples. Father waited anxiously for the appearance of the Men's Brotherhood, hoping that their remembrance would be in cash, but it wasn't; they contributed a leather chair.

By noon the tables overflowed with presents: handmade lace, wearing apparel, preserved fruits, cakes, candies, oranges, nine scarves, four pairs of mittens, and for father seven pairs of knitted socks with ties to match. The gifts were tokens of love from men and women who had no other way of expressing their gratitude and devotion to the pastor who counseled them, freed their children from escapades, solved their domestic problems, found employment for them, and lent them money when he had it.

The lace, for example, that Sister Hawkins had been tatting since August had a story in it. Joe Hawkins, a farmer, had been stricken with a ruptured appendix just as the oats ripened. Father had managed the farm, helped to harvest the crop, and put up hay that would have been ruined by imminent rain. Joe Hawkins' hired man said the parson should have been a farmer, and that was reward enough for father. Mrs. Hawkins had spent every spare moment since on the lace.

The story of the six jars of plum butter from Mrs. Aiken was ten months old. The previous March Mrs. Aiken had contracted diphtheria and had been taken to the County Hospital for Contagious Diseases. Father had sent the Ladies Aid to the rescue, and their volunteers had kept the Aiken house running and the three children and husband fed until the mother could return. Daily father had called on her at the hospital, delivered letters to her from her family, and bolstered her spirits. One day when she said, "Oh, Mr. Spence, I'll never be able to thank you," he had laughted it off. "You just make me some plum butter next summer, and we'll be even." She had put up the butter, all right; it was her Christmas gift.

People who were that generous with their preacher did not forget his children. We received candy enough to last, with careful hoarding, for six weeks or more and many games, which father inspected carefully to be sure that they could not be utilized for gambling. When he carried one to the furnace, we didn't mind; what was one among a dozen?

*—Get Thee Behind Me* 1942

# ICICLES

Icicles hang from the church steeple, inverted spires. They glitter in the sun, ethereal red and blue, more fine-cut, more exquisite, than the spire of Salisbury.

# CHRISTMAS WEATHER

The little town on the white slopes is like a Christmas card—red church, white roofs, and smoking chimneys; and at night, above the gold window panes, a blue glitter of stars.

 # CHRISTMAS TREE

Out on the lawn, the fir stands all sparkling-white, and a big star at its tip—and I know how Christmas trees are born!

\* \* \* Ruth Suckow 1919

* * * Susan Glaspell

# Cherished and Shared of Old

HANK GOODNESS for the snow, thought Addie Morrison, as she watched the two children racing round the barn. And she was thinking it was nice there were some things that were everywhere—most everywhere: like sun and rain, like wind and the snow, *so's* when you were sent far from your home there were these things—like the stars—to make you feel a little more at home in a distant land.

"Not a soul here they ever knew before," she would think of these two little Dutch children she'd taken into her home. They were warm now at night—not wandering on a road. They weren't hungry now—mercy no, she'd seen to *that*, but what are they *thinking*, she'd wonder, as at times they'd sit there so gravely. She wished they'd do more things they shouldn't, for when you're too good you must be a little afraid.

She hadn't been able to stand the pictures in the papers—so many tired children wanting to get back home. Her daughter Emmey, in the East, was working for little ones who had been turned out into the world by the misfortunes of this war in Europe. "Mother dear," she wrote, "I can't get home this Christmas—just can't. But I could send you two children for whom you could make a Christmas—the way you used to for me and Jack. You'll be so sorry for Johanna and Piet, and come to love them; perhaps you'll want them to stay on there with you in our old home. There were always children on the Morrison place."

So once more there were children on the old Morrison place, but could she make a happy Christmas for this little girl and boy bereft of their own? She could say "Merry Christmas," but could she make their hearts glad? And what is Christmas if there is not warmth within? "Maybe *you'll* help," she was saying to the turkey she crammed with savory stuffing. "And what about you?" she thought, regarding with favor the mince pies on the shelf.

She didn't even know what they were used to for Christmas. She wished, for just five minutes, she could talk to their mother. "What would they like?" she'd ask. And their mother would reply—eagerly, so anxious: "Oh, if you would give them—" But this mother couldn't speak up for her children—struck down trying to hurry them to safety.

Germans did that. The Schultzes were Germans—over there in their fine house on the hill. And so her heart hardened anew against Emma Schultz—and that was good, for she found it not so easy to hate Emma at Christmas.

Never a Christmas they hadn't shared—all those years they were growing up. In this very kitchen they'd hung around sniffing and tasting. And when they weren't here they were at the Schultzes'. She had two homes—her own and Schultzes'. And Emma had two—her own and the Morrisons'.

And then they had to act like that! Just to get a piece of land that didn't belong to them at all they'd fought John Morrison, best friend they'd had since they came—greenhorns—into this country. Country where the Morrisons had been since first there were white men in Iowa! Not to her dying day would she forget her father's face that late afternoon he came back from town, and standing by this very table said: "Well, they've won. The court has given them the strip. Don't ask me why. I don't know why. But I do know this! They've won the land—but they've lost the Morrisons. Never again—do you hear me, Addie?—never again can a Morrison be friend to a Schultz."

Oh, she heard him all right, and never forgot. How could she forget, when she saw him change from that day? The land wasn't so very important. But the defeat—bitter words spoken—from that day he began to brood, until soon people were saying: "Why Addie, seems like your father is beginning to fail."

But Emil Schultz—*he* didn't fail. As the Morrisons began to have less and less, the Schultzes had more and more. Emma Schultz's land-grabbing father lived on till just last year—and many a snow had fallen since they carried John Morrison to the last land he would know.

So a fine daughter *she* was—letting into her heart memories of those long ago Christmases with Emma Schultz. Memories were tricky things—come Christmastime. Maybe it was because you went on doing the same things. You made the cranberry sauce, trimmed the tree—doing alone the little things you'd done with someone else—with the dearest friend you'd ever had.

For no one had ever taken Emma's place. Who could take the place of the friend with whom you'd shared all those good years of your life? Emma helped her make all her wedding things. Emma was there when her first baby was born. She'd named that daughter Emma. Later she'd thought of changing it—but not easy to change a name, and anyway she had an aunt named Emma—she got around it that way. And Walter. Emma was to have married Addie's brother Walter. But Walter went away to war—that other time the Germans tried to wreck the world—and he never came back. And they had comforted each other then.

Yes, laughter and sorrow they had shared. And how divided now! That fought-over land connected the Morrison and Schultz farms. Connected only to divide. It wasn't land—it was a gulf, a gulf that had widened with the years. Feeling—that is what lives on. You might even have forgotten what caused it, but it has come to have a life of its own, regardless of what it flamed from long ago. That is why there is hate in the world—(she half knew this, tried not to know)—hate unreasoning, living on because, one way or other, it got there in the first place; and when a thing has existed a long time it gives you the idea you can't change it—even makes you think you don't want to.

The smells of Christmas brought Emma close to her—Christmas smells trying to make her betray the legacy of hate to which she had been so bitterly loyal! And what if we *did* get many a Christmas dinner together, she thought. Remember the *words*—those very words they spoke!

Yes—the words. How cruel—and again how blessed—were words. They could carry testimony of love, the sympathy that brought heart closer to heart and warmed the world. And they could blast and wound and kill like those contraptions of the devil man used against man in war. And their life was as long as the life of man.

Longer. For the men who had fought for that land were gone now—her father and Emma's. Walter was gone, and Addie's husband. Her children were in homes of their own and she lived on here at the old place—running down now, and she couldn't do anything about that—and over there on the hill, in her fine new house, lived Emma Schultz. She had a frigidaire, they said—a vacuum and everything to make life easy. She wore a sealskin coat and was proud and cold—how she'd laugh if she knew poor old Addie Morrison was thinking of the days they'd made the Christmas candy together—remembering how Emma's stocking hung at the Morrisons', and Addie's at the Schultzes'.

"Come in and get warm!" she called to the children. "Stamp hard! Shake!" she cried gaily. They got in a mix-up getting off Piet's ski pants. "You take one leg and I'll take the other," she said to Johanna. Johanna was the little mother, two years older than Piet, who was four. Addie made a great fuss about this, pretending she couldn't pull so hard, letting on she was going to fall over backward, until Piet laughed out loud and Johanna smiled—her grave little smile that seemed to be feeling its way. "It will take time," Addie told herself. Tomorrow they'd have their presents—sleds and skates, toys and new caps and mufflers and mittens. And tomorrow the Allen children were coming over to play with them. Once she heard them break out in laughter that came because it couldn't help itself—how happy she'd be, as if a little of the weight of misery had lifted from the world. Perhaps Christmas could do that. That was what Christmas was for. She wanted them to be happy as she hadn't wanted anything in years. That would be *her* Christmas present—a smile not uncertain, a laugh that was happy clear to the inside. People like Schultzes running little children out of their homes! As for her, she was an *American*. She didn't hold with such things. (And way in her heart Addie Morrison knew Emma Schultz didn't hold with them either—but this she couldn't let herself know.)

Well if that little fellow wasn't edging up to the cookie-jar. Good! You must think it's *your* house when you go after the cookie-jar.

Johanna said, in her new careful English, "Thank you," for the cookie; little Piet said something she didn't understand, but he smiled and she knew it was "Thank you."

What funny little cookies the Schultzes used to make for Christmas. Cut in all sorts of shapes—a rabbit, a star, a St. Nicholas and something called a grampus, and supposed to be for the bad child, but it had currants and nuts in it just the same, so who cared? Perhaps

Johanna and Piet were used to cookies like that. Yes, Emma might know more than she did about what these children were used to. But Emma—warm in a fine sealskin coat—what did *she* care?

"Oh—pret-ty," she heard Johanna murmur, and turned to find her fingering a length of red ribbon that was to be tied on the tree.

Addie stood stock-still watching her, for the little girl's fingers moved over the bright stuff so wistfully, as if—as if she had once loved something like this. "Oh you poor little thing," she thought, in a new wave of sympathy and tenderness—anger too. All the little fineries left behind. Only what you needed—not the pretty things to make life gay.

"Time to dress ourselves up for Christmas," she said, slipping the bright broad ribbon under the collar of Johanna's sweater and making a fine red bow.

And then she began to laugh—Emma running after a *pig*, trying to catch the pig to tie a red ribbon round his neck. That was one of the crazy things they did together—dressing up the animals for Christmas. Well Emma caught the pig, but fell down doing it and Emma and pig rolled over and over together—the pig squirming and Emma clutching. Addie could see them now and she went on laughing, until the children, thinking there must be something very funny indeed, politely joined in.

The snow continued to fall softly, knowing it was Christmas and the world should be white, and after the dinner things were cleared away Addie wondered whether they'd like to be bundled up and go out again. That was the trouble—it was still hard to know for sure what they would like, for it wasn't *their* house yet.

But suddenly it was! What in the world were they looking at out that window—dancing up and down, catching hold of each other and squealing and pointing?

Oh—*dear. Now* what? For there he was—that miserable Schultz dog who came bounding over as if he didn't know a Schultz shouldn't come to the Morrisons'. She started for the door to go chase him away but the children thought she was going to let him in, and they were right upon her, all excited and happy—*natural*—for the first time they really were children. And all because that ugly Schultz dog—for some crazy reason called Doc—was standing there wagging his tail as if waiting for them to come out and play with him.

"Bad dog," she said. "German. Bad German dog,"—though she knew she shouldn't be doing this.

But they didn't care. It didn't seem to make any difference to them that Doc was German. And then Addie knew. It wasn't only the ribbons and the toys had been left behind. The dog had been left behind too. . . .

"We'll get a dog," she said. "A nice dog. This is the homeliest dog ever lived."

And Doc was a very funny-looking dog. He wasn't *any* kind of dog—just Doc. He had a bulldog face and crooked legs, but he was sort of a dog of all nations, and Addie knew in her heart that the kindness of all nations came together in Doc, and that Doc was a *good* dog. But he was a Schultz.

She tried to interest them in the dog they would have, but they wanted Doc and wanted him right now; and as Addie saw that first flare-up of joy begin to die down into disappointment, of course she couldn't stand it and there began a mad gay scramble to get them into their clothes so they could rush out and play with Doc Schultz.

Then she remembered they were used to having dogs draw things—pictures of Holland always had dogs drawing little carts—so she hurried into the shut-up front room, where the presents waited in secret, to get the Christmas sled—for might as well be killed for a sheep as a lamb, she thought.

Oh they were so delighted! They could scarcely wait to get out—and then they were all in a scramble together, Doc jumping on them and waving his silly tail—and for goodness sakes if the dog didn't seem to be *grinning*—and the children were laughing and screaming and they all went tearing away together.

And Addie Morrison sat there thinking it was strange—so very strange—that their first happy moment on the Morrison place came through Emma Schultz. She sat there alone remembering her dogs and Emma's—new sleds and other mad scrambles in the Christmas snow.

Emma Schultz was remembering something herself. She was again a little girl not eight—new to America, a greenhorn. And the children at school stared and laughed at her because she talked funny and didn't know their ways. But little Addie Morrison—so pretty then—came up and hooked her arm through Emma's and said: "You and me, lets us be friends."

More than anything else in the world she would like to walk over to Addie Morrison now, open the kitchen door just as she used to, and say—"You and me, lets us be friends."

At Christmas it was so hard not to remember. And this Christmas most of all, because again—after all these years—Addie was befriending the stranger. How good of Addie! How good of America! And she wondered if anyone could love America as did the one who had come here a stranger and been taken in.

*She* was the one to do something for these children, for who could know better than she what it was to be a child among things not familiar.

She was putting in a big jar the *lebkuchen*, German Christmas cookies she made every year. She wouldn't have had the heart to make them this year, but her mother hadn't many Christmases left and clung to the things she was used to. Next week Emma's Sunday-school class would come for their party, and they'd have these cookies and their presents. But it was lonely here today.

Ten thousand times she'd wished that land in the bottom of the sea. What is land, compared to the love of friends? How gladly she would have given it back. It had changed things for the Schultzes. Her father grew hard after that and wanted to make money and didn't care about friends. And she herself had to pretend she didn't care, and that made one hard too. The Schultzes didn't like being told they weren't Americans, being shouted at they weren't honest. They'd show them who the Schultzes were! But it had been lonely business, and at Christmas especially she knew there still lived in her heart all she and Addie had loved together, dear things shared. She'd like to cross that strip—and abolish it in crossing—open the kitchen door and see if there wasn't something she could do for these little children against whom a wicked wrong had been worked. But what nonsense. You couldn't change the way things were, and Addie had grown more bitter with the years. She'd *shut* the door—shut it in Emma Schultz's face.

"Emma! I hear Doc barking," her mother called out to her. "He wants to come in."

She opened her own kitchen door, and yes—there stood Doc. But—*what in the world?* He was all decorated for Christmas. Red ribbon was wound round his collar and tied in a big gay bow. Now who could have done *that?*

And suddenly Emma Schultz sat down—so sure there was only

one person in the world could have sent Doc home decorated for Christmas. She and Addie used to do that together. The dogs always had their big red Christmas bows. Addie had not forgotten! Oh, she had sent a message saying she remembered. And Emma Schultz began hurrying fast as she could—getting the cookies—presents for those she had for her Sunday-school class—for couldn't she get others for them?—filling a big basket, hurrying into her boots, her coat, and out into the snow. It was Christmas! She ran across the strip giving it scarcely a thought, so eager to get to the Morrisons'.

But at the kitchen door she paused. So many years . . . Then she knocked, and Addie opened the door.

"Why—why Emma *Schultz*," she said, as if she didn't know what to say.

"Merry Christmas, Addie," said Emma—timidly, bravely.

"Why—why—" And then all of a sudden Addie cried: "Merry Christmas yourself!"—and swiftly added: "For pity sakes come right in out of the snow!"

A little later they were all sitting round the kitchen stove, nibbling the cookies Emma had brought, Emma and Addie drinking tea and the children their cocoa—so cozy in the Morrison kitchen. Yes, Johanna and Piet knew cookies like these, and great fun they had picking out now a new moon, now a little man—Johanna hugging the doll Emma had brought and Piet dangling the baby panda.

"Emma!" Addie burst out with a laugh—"do you remember the *pig?*"

While they were laughing came a barking and scratching at the door and Johanna and Piet ran to let in their friend Doc.

As the children were busy brushing him off, Emma said, very low: "Oh, Addie—when he came home all fixed up for Christmas—and I knew you had remembered—were telling me you remembered—"

Addie had been sitting with her back to Doc. She turned now, and saw that the bow she had tied on Johanna at this moment adorned Emma's dog Doc.

And Emma thought she had done this! A Schultz thought a Morrison had made the first move.

Ah, there was danger in that moment—danger the world has faced time and again. Old bitter loyalties—resentments of many years—right there, ready to rush in.

But something else came flooding into that moment: It was the children had done this. The children whom hate had driven here—brought love. How strange that this could be. Like a miracle it seemed.

She was afraid she was going to cry, so when Doc came sniffing up to the stove she said, almost crossly: "Why Emma Schultz—that dog's hungry."

"I'll tell you, children," she went on, "what do you say we give him our beef stew, for tomorrow we'll have turkey."

Doc knew it was to be for him and was dancing all around, his big bow bobbing. "Say Merry Christmas!" cried Addie, holding high the plate. Doc waved a hearty "Merry Christmas"—and they all watched Doc Schultz devour the Morrison stew.

The children clapped their hands at the speed with which he cleaned the plate. Emma and Addie smiled at each other—so much alive and warm between them. Dogs of other years were wearing their Christmas bows and cleaning the plate. In a changing world of many sorrows it can be sad to remember alone. But when friends share dear memories—a fire in the cold, light in the darkness.

And right there the children began a great clatter, running round in circles with Doc. Why they weren't a *bit* afraid—for all the world as if they knew something had happened there amongst them. Whether they knew it or not, it was true—how blessed and true—that fear flew out through the window when love came in by the door.

"SCHOOL OUT ALREADY? MY, YOU TEACHERS CERTAINLY GET A LONG CHRISTMAS VACATION."

* * * Paul Engle

# Christmas on the Farm

VERY Christmas should begin with the sound of bells, and when I was a child mine always did. But they were sleigh bells, not church bells, for we lived in a part of Cedar Rapids, Iowa, where there were no churches. My bells were on my father's team of horses as he drove up to our horse-headed hitcing post with the bobsled that would take us to celebrate Christmas on the family farm ten miles out in the country. My father would bring the team down Fifth Avenue at a smart trot, flicking his whip over the horses' rumps and making the bells double their light, thin jangling over the snow, whose radiance threw back a brilliance like the sound of bells.

Whose father now drives up on Christmas morning in such exciting style as mine did when I was a child?

With more anticipation than we would have today waiting for a jet to fly in from Paris, my younger sister and I would stand at a window looking down the street. Kathryn would clap her hands, jump up and down, and cry "There he comes!"

Such speed, such power, it seemed, such a roar of arrival with the runners crunching on the snow, the bells clanging, the horses snorting as father snapped his long whip over their heads! How dull the rubber-skidded arrival of a plane, compared to the rush and clang of steel runners beautifully sliding over ice and snow.

Father would bring the bobsled smartly around in a whirl of snow and prancing feet in the sort of arrival which no plane on a runway and no car on a plowed and paved street could ever imitate. By then my sister and I would have run out to help, holding the reins between us as father tied the team to our hitching post. There was more feeling of motion and flight in our two horsepower, Billy and Buck, than in any hundreds of mechanical horsepower.

Our whole Christmas was that way; there was more life in it, close to animals and to the land, than in our city celebration today. Like most people toward the beginning of this troubled century, we had relatives on the farm.

There are no such departures as ours for that farm any more: the whole family piling into the bobsled with a foot of golden oat straw to lie in and heavy buffalo robes to lie under, the horses stamping the soft snow, and at every motion of their hoofs the bells jingling, jingling. My father sat there with the reins firmly held, wearing a long coat made from the hide of a favorite family horse, the deep chestnut color still glowing, his mittens also from the same hide. It always troubled me as a boy of eight that the horses had so indifferent a view of their late friend appearing as a warm overcoat on the back of the man who put the iron bit in their mouths.

A bobsled was the wonderful and proper way to travel on Christmas morning. The space it offered was generous, like the holiday itself. There was no crowding on narrow seats where children had to sit upright. Instead, the long, wide body allowed us such comfort and freedom as no car or plane can give.

In that abundant dimension, we could burrow down under the clean-smelling straw, pull a shaggy robe over us, and travel warm and snug while still being outdoors with the wind in our faces.

We could hop out and ride on the heavy runners, the snow piling up against our boots and the runners making it seem dangerous as they bounced and twisted over the unpaved streets, making their hissing, tearing sound over the packed snow.

As the runners slid over snow, ice, and an occasional stone or bare spot with dirt, they would carry on a sustained monologue continually changing. They would whisper gently over snow, mutter angrily over ice, squeak over gravel, cry in rage over an exposed rock, then go back to the long rhythm of the glide over hard-packed snow.

That was dramatic travel, just as the horses, alive and individual, each with its own characteristics, were a more exciting source of motive power than a mechanical engine with its stink and noise.

We were close to those horses. My father had bought them young and trained them himself, so that he could drive them with a light hand, as much by the expressive sound of his voice as by a whip on the withers or a bit in the mouth. We would continually urge Billy along as he lagged just enough behind Buck so that he had a little less to pull.

On a level piece of road, Father would collect the reins firmly, cluck to the team, snap the whip over their ears, and settle them into a fast trot, bells jangling in celebration, runners clacking, and the children yelling with the speed and sway of it.

There are no streets like those any more: the snow sensibly left on the road for the sake of sleighs and easy travel. And along the streets we met other horses, so that we moved from one set of bells to another, from the tiny tinkle of the individual bells on the shafts to the silvery leaping sound of the long strands hung over the harness. There would be an occasional brass-mounted automobile laboring on its narrow tires and as often as not pulled up the slippery hills by a horse, and we would pass it with a triumphant shout for an awkward nuisance which was obviously not here to stay.

The country road ran through a landscape of little hills and shallow valleys and heavy groves of timber, including one of the great towering black walnut trees which were all cut down a year later to be made into gunstocks for the First World War. The great moment was when we left the road and turned up the long lane on the farm. It ran through fields where watermelons were always planted in the summer because of the fine sandy soil, and I could go out and break one open to see its Christmas colors of green skin and red inside. My grandfather had been given some of that farm as bounty land for service as a cavalryman in the Civil War.

My uncle, mother's brother, and our cousins lived on the same place where mother had been born. Somehow, a place of country quiet, with livestock crunching on its feed, with sheds and barns and corncribs, with crop and pasture land rolling away serenely, their shape clearer in winter under the defining snow, seemed the best of all possible places to celebrate this holiday begun in a little village in sheepraising country on the other side of the world.

Near the low house on the hill, with oaks on one side and apple trees on the other, my father would stand up, flourish his whip, and bring the bobsled right up to the door of the house with a burst of speed.

There are no such arrivals any more: the harness bells ringing and clashing, the horses whinnying at the horses in the barn and receiving a great trumpeting whinny in reply, the dogs leaping into the bobsled and burrowing under the buffalo robes, a squawking from the hen house, a yelling of "Whoa, whoa," at the excited horses, boy and girl cousins howling around the bobsled, and the descent into the snow with the Christmas basket carried by my mother.

My Uncle Charlie was certainly not John the Baptist wearing a coat of camel's hair and a leather girdle about his loins. Nor was he preaching "Repent ye; for the kingdom of heaven is at hand."

But standing at the farmhouse door, wearing a heavy sheepskin jacket over his stained overalls, urging us in with a hearty shout of, "Come and set where it's warm," he was certainly a prophet. What he prophesied was good cheer and a gay Christmas.

Charlie had the gentle dispostion of a saint and the shoulders of a professional wrestler. He had once stayed five minutes in a ring at the county fair with a champion known with cruel candor as "The Strangler."

As I went in, he would give my arm a friendly twist and say in great confidence, lowering his voice to make me feel that I too was a pretty good country wrestler, "After dinner we'll go down to the haymow and I'll show you how to break out of a hammer lock."

After mother, the girls and the baskets had been rushed into the house by our cousins, and the dogs persuaded out of the straw, we would go on to the barn. Charlie would help father unhitch the team and take them into stalls, where they could see the horses which had been whinnying at them in suspicious welcome.

A barn was the most wonderful place for a child to begin Christmas Day, the same sort of place where that first Day took place. Here were the snorts and stampings and mutterings of livestock, the yowling of cats waiting for the saucer of milk. It was a modest barn, but rich with abundant life, and the mangers were filled with nourishment for that life.

The children of those countries which celebrate it are fortunate to have Christmas, but I was lucky beyond most children to have my day begin at a cheerful barn on a low hill in the prairie, where the animals and I could look across the snowy country and be glad we were inside.

That winter odor of a barn is a wonderfully complex one, rich and warm and utterly unlike the smell of the same barn in summer: the body heat of many animals weighing a thousand pounds and more; pigs in one corner making their dark, brown-sounding grunts; milk cattle still nuzzling the manger for wisps of hay; horses eying the newcomers and rolling their deep, oval eyes white; oats, hay, and straw tangy still with the live

August sunlight; the manure steaming; the sharp odor of leather harness rubbed with neat's-foot oil to keep it supple; the molasses-sweet odor of ensilage in the silo where the fodder was almost fermenting. It is a smell from strong and living things, and my father always said it was the secret of health, that it scoured out a man's lungs; and he would stand there, breathing deeply, one hand on a horse's rump, watching the steam come out from under the blankets as the team cooled down from their rapid trop up the lane. It gave him a better appetite, he argued, than plain fresh air, which was thin and had no body to it.

By the time we reached the house my mother and sisters were wearing aprons and busying in the kitchen, as red-faced as the women who had been there all morning. The kitchen was the biggest room in the house and all family life save sleeping went on there. The kitchen range was a tremendous black and gleaming one called a Smoke Eater, with pans bubbling over the holes above the firebox and reservoir of hot water at the side, lined with dull copper, from which my uncle would dip a basin of water and shave above the sink, turning his lathered face now and then to drop a remark into the women's talk, waving his straight-edged razor as if it were a threat to make them believe him. My job was to go to the woodpile out back and keep the fire burning, splitting the chunks of oak and hickory, watching how cleanly the ax went through the tough wood.

The tree was brought out from town, and on it were many paper ornaments made by my cousins, as well as beautiful ones brought from the Black Forest, where the family had originally lived. There were popcorn balls, from corn planted on the sunny slope next to the watermelons, paper horns with homemade candy, and apples from the orchard. The gifts tended to be hand-knit socks, or wool ties, or fancy crocheted "yokes" for nightgowns, tatted collars for blouses, doilies with fancy flower patterns for tables, tidies for chairs, and once I received a brilliantly polished cow horn with a cavalryman crudely but bravely carved on it. And there would usually be a cornhusk doll, perhaps with a prune or walnut for a face, and a gay dress of old corset-cover scrap with its ribbons still bright. And there were real candles burning with real flames, every guest sniffing the air for the smell of scorching pine needles. No electrically lit tree has the warm and primitive presence of a tree with a crown of living fires over it, suggesting whatever true flame Joseph may have kindled on that original cold night.

There are no dinners like that any more: every item from the farm itself, with no deep-freezer, no car for driving into town for packaged food. The pies had been baked the day before, pumpkin, apple, and mince; as we ate them, we could look out the window and see the cornfield where the pumpkins grew, the trees from which the apples were picked. There was cottage cheese, with the dripping bags of curds still hanging from the cold cellar ceiling. The bread had been baked that morning, heating up the oven for the meat, and as my aunt hurried by I could smell in her apron the freshest of all odors with which the human nose is honored — bread straight from the oven. There would be a huge brown crock of beans with smoked pork from the hog butchered every November. We would see, beyond the crock, the broad black iron kettle in a corner of the barnyard, turned upside down, the innocent hogs stopping to scratch on it.

There would be every form of preserve: wild grape from the vines in the grove, crabapple jelly, wild blackberry and tame raspberry, strawberry from the bed in the garden, sweet and sour pickles with dill from the edge of the lane where it grew wild, pickles from the rind of the same watermelon we had cooled in the tank at the milkhouse and eaten on a hot September afternoon.

Cut into the slope of the hill behind the house, with a little door of its own, was the vegetable cellar, from which came carrots, turnips, cabbages, potatoes, squash. Sometimes my scared cousins were sent there for punishment, to sit in the darkness and meditate on their sins; but never on Christmas Day. For days after such an ordeal, they could not endure biting into a carrot.

And of course there was the traditional sauerkraut, with flecks of caraway seed. I remember one Christmas Day, when a ten-gallon crock of it in the basement, with a stone weighting down the lid, had blown up, driving the stone against the floor of the parlor, and my uncle had exclaimed, "Good God, the piano's fallen through the floor."

All the meat was from the home place too. Turkey, of course, and most useful of all, the goose — the very one which had chased me the summer before, hissing and darting out its bill at the end of its curving neck like a feathered snake. Here was the universal bird of an older Christmas: its down was plucked, washed, and hung in bags in the barn to be put into pillows; its awkward body was roasted until the skin was crisp as a fine paper; and the grease from its carcass was melted down, a little camphor added, and rubbed on the chests of coughing children. We ate, slept on, and wore that goose.

The most tantalizing odor of all was the sour goose. This was an old family tradition brought from Germany, and was Charlie's favorite eating. For many families the typical tone of Christmas was the sweetness of cake and candy. For us, it was the splendid sourness of vinegar poured over a cooking goose, the acid fumes tickling our delighted noses.

This was Aunt Minnie's specialty, I suppose because she seemed to have as much vinegar in her veins as blood, and a tongue as sharp as the fork with which she tested the goose.

Minnie was thin and sharp in her features, too, and I can see her bending over that plump goose and stabbing it with her fork to see whether the skin was crisp, almost as if she resented any creature which was so fat it made her own skinniness more apparent. In the bottom of the pan, vinegar and grease bubbled happily together, Minnie scooping up the pungent broth and basting the goose with it.

When serving the sour goose, Charlie would put a large piece on my plate and say, "Eat hearty, boy, that goose will put wire in your muscles."

I believed him, and I bit into the meat with its biting taste. In a few years Charlie was gone, there was no more sour goose, and my muscles have been softer ever since.

I was blessed as a child with a remote uncle from the nearest railroad town, Uncle Ben, who was admiringly referred to as a "railroad man," working the run into Omaha. Ben had been to Chicago; just often enough, as his wife Minnie said with a sniff in her voice, "to ruin the fool, not often enough to teach him anything useful." Ben refused to eat fowl in any form, and as a Christmas token a little pork roast would be put in the oven just for him, always referred to by the hurrying ladies in the kitchen as "Ben's chunk." Ben would make frequent trips to the milkhouse, returning each time a little redder in the face, usually with one of the men toward whom he had jerked his head. It was not many years before I came to associate Ben's remarkably fruity breath not only with the mince pie, but with the jug I found sunk in the bottom of the cooling tank with a stone tied to its neck. He was a romantic person in my life for his constant travels and for that dignifying term "railroad man," so much more impressive than farmer or lawyer. Yet now I see that he was a short man with a fine natural shyness, giving us knives and guns because he had no children of his own.

And of course the trimmings were from the farm too: the hickory nut cake made with nuts gathered in the grove after the first frost and hulled out by my cousins with yellowed hands; the black walnut cookies, sweeter than any taste; the fudge with butternuts crowding it. In the mornings we would be given a hammer, a flatiron, and a bowl of nuts to crack and pick out for the homemade ice cream.

And there was the orchard beyond the kitchen window, the Wealthy, the Russet, the Wolf with its giant-sized fruit, and an apple romantically called the Northern Spy as if it were a suspicious character out of the Civil War.

All families had their special Christmas food. Ours was called Dutch Bread, made from a dough halfway between bread and cake, stuffed with citron and every sort of nut from the farm — hazel, black walnut, hickory, butternut. A little round one was always baked for me in Clabber Girl baking soda can, and my last act on Christmas Eve was to put it by the tree so that Santa Claus would find it and have a snack — after all, he'd come a long, cold way to our house. And every Christmas morning he would have eaten it. My aunt made the same Dutch Bread and we smeared over it the same butter she had been churning from their own Jersey (highest butter-fat content) cream that same morning.

To eat in the same room where food is cooked — that is the way to thank the Lord for His abundance. The long table, with its different levels where additions had been made for the small fry, ran the length of the kitchen. The air was heavy with odors not only of food on plates but of the act of cooking itself, along with the metallic smell of heated iron from the hard-working Smoke Eater, and the whole stove offered us its yet uneaten prospects of more goose and untouched pies. To see the giblet gravy made and poured into a gravy boat, which had painted on its sides winter scenes of boys sliding and deer bounding over snow, is the surest way to overeat its swimming richness.

The warning for Christmas dinner was always an order to go to the milkhouse for cream, where we skinmmed from the cooling pans of fresh milk the cream which had the same golden color as the flanks of the Jersey cows which had given it. The last deed before eating was grinding the coffee beans in the little mill, adding that exotic odor to the more native ones of goose and spiced pumpkin pie. Then all would sit at the table and my uncle would ask the grace, sometimes in German, but later, for the benefit of us ignorant children, in English:

> *Come, Lord Jesus, be our guest,*
> *Share this food that you have blessed.*

There are no blessings like that any more: every scrap of food for which my uncle had asked the blessing was the result of his own hard work. What he took to the Lord for Him to make holy was the plain substance that an Iowa farm could produce in an average year with decent rainfall and proper plowing and manure.

The first act of dedication on such a Christmas was to the occasion which had begun it, thanks to the Child of a pastoral couple who no doubt knew a good deal about rainfall and grass and the fattening of animals. The second act of dedication was to the ceremony of eating. My aunt kept a turmoil of food circulating, and to refuse any of it was somehow to violate the elevated nature of the day. We were there not only to celebrate a fortunate event for mankind but also to recognize that suffering is the natural lot of men—and to consume the length and breadth of that meal was to suffer! But we all faced the ordeal with courage. Uncle Ben would let out his belt—a fancy western belt with steer heads and silver buckle—with a snap and a sigh. The women managed better by always getting up from the table and trotting to the kitchen sink or the Smoke Eater or outdoors for some item left in the cold. The men sat there grimly enduring the glory of their appetites.

After dinner, late in the afternoon, the women would make despairing gestures toward the dirty dishes and scoop up hot water from the reservoir at the side of the range. The men would go to the barn and look after the livestock. My older cousin would take his new .22 rifle and stalk out across the pasture with the remark, "I saw that fox just now looking for his Christmas goose." Or sleds would be dragged out and we would slide in a long snake, feet hooked into the sled behind, down the hill and across the westward sloping fields into the sunset. Bones would be thrown to dogs, suet tied in the oak trees for the juncos and winter-defying chickadees, a saucer of skimmed milk set out for the cats, daintily and disgustedly picking their padded feet through the snow, and crumbs scattered on a bird feeder where already the crimson cardinals would be dropping out of the sky like blood. Then back to the house for a final warming up before leaving.

There was usually a song around the tree before we were all bundled up, many thanks all around for gifts, the basket as loaded as when it came, more so, for leftover food had been piled in it. My father and uncle would have brought up the team from the barn and hooked them into the double shafts of the bobsled, and we would all go out into the freezing air of early evening.

On the way to the door I would walk under a photograph of my grandfather, his cavalry saber hung over it. (I had once sneaked it down from the wall and in a burst of gallantry had killed a mouse with it behind the corncrib.) With his long white beard he loked like one of the prophets in Hurlbut's illustrated *Story of the Bible,* and it was years before I discovered that as a young man he had not been off fighting the Philistines but the painted Sioux. It was hard to think of that gentle man, whose family had left Germany in protest over military service, swinging that deadly blade and yelling in a cavalry charge. But he had done just that, in some hard realization that sometimes the way to have peace and a quiet life on a modest farm was to go off and fight for them.

And now those bells again as the horses, impatient from their long standing in the barn, stamped and shook their harness, my father holding them back with a soft clucking in his throat and a hard pull on the reins. The smell of wood smoke flavoring the air in our noses, the cousins shivering with cold, "Good-by, good-by," called out from everyone, and the bobsled would slide off, creaking over the frost-brittle snow. All of us, my mother included, would dig down in the straw and pull the buffalo robes up to our chins. As the horses settled into a steady trot, the bells gently chiming in their rhythmical beat, we would fall half asleep, the hiss of the runners comforting. As we looked up to the night sky through half-closed eyelids, the constant bounce and swerve of the runners would seem to shake the little stars as if they would fall into our laps. But that one great star in the East never wavered. Nothing could shake it from the sky as we drifted home on Christmas.

* * * Susan Allen Toth

# The Cut-Glass Christmas

HE DECEMBER after my father died, when I was seven and my sister was nine, we worried about Mother. We knew she was going to feel bad on Christmas Day, and we wanted to do something special but we didn't know what it could be. We huddled in the bathroom, whispered in corners, argued intensely in our bedroom after lights out and — unusual for us — at last came to an agreement. We would be Mother's Santa; we would fill a stocking for her just as she did for us. How surprised she'd be on Christmas morning to see her very own stocking hanging there on a drawer pull of the maple bureau in our living room! We felt sure that would cheer her up.

A week before Christmas we emptied our piggy banks and set out for Woolworth's, where we always bought our presents. Woolworth's was the Santa-Claus-and-Christmas-tree part of Christmas. It blazed with lights in the after-school dark, smelled of peanuts and popcorn at a counter heaped for the season with chocolate-covered cherries and cellophane-wrapped, red-and-white candy canes, rang with "Jingle Bells" and "Hark! the Herald" on a radio turned up loud near the cash register. Ever year we each were allowed to pick out one new ornament from the tree-trimming counter, where we fondled brilliant glass balls, folding tissue-paper bells, and colored electric lights that bubbled when you plugged them in. No other store in our small Iowa town had the glitter and gleam that Woolworth's had at Christmas.

First we headed for our two traditional counters for Mother's presents — cosmetics and kitchen utensils. Although Mother never wore makeup, I wouldn't give up hope, encouraging her with a fake tortoise-shell compact of red rouge or a tiny bottle of Evening in Paris perfume or a set of mascara brushes. My sister was fond of small silver funnels, metal straining spoons, glass measuring cups. But this Christmas we felt none of our usual gifts would be quite right for a special stocking. We wandered up and down the rows, pondering pencil sharpeners, packaged stationery in floral cardboard boxes, little china dogs that were really salt and pepper shakers. We rejected a card of assorted needles from England, a fat red pincushion with an attached strawberry-shaped emery ball, an earring tree. The tree was gold-colored metal and spun on a plastic base, but unfortunately, our mother did not wear earrings.

At last we found ourselves together, discouraged, at a back counter, hidden behind toys and semidarkened under a burned-out fluorescent light, where Woolworth's kept its glasses, dishes, pots and pans. We knew we couldn't afford a teakettle or a frying pan. Mother used empty jam jars for glasses and she didn't need any more silverware. But suddenly we both saw at the far end of the counter a section of cut-glass dishes—not just plain round cereal bowls, but jagged and deeply carved, dark-green glass. Small bowls were ten cents; a size big enough for soup or oatmeal was 20. I hurried to the end of the counter, where it was brighter. How the glass shone! My sister agreed that the fancy dishes were unlike anything Mother had. With our allowances pooled, we could buy six small bowls and two big ones. The clerk at the front packed the dishes carefully in newspaper and warned us to unpack them gently. The edges were sharp, she said. We hurried home in the dark, happy and warm inside with our secret. Eight cut-glass bowls! Mother would never have had such a Christmas!

On Christmas Eve my sister and I faced our only other problem— what to use for Mother's stocking. We each had a red felt Christmas stocking, hung year after year, but we hadn't had enough money to buy one for Mother. While she was washing dishes after supper, we tiptoed down the hall to her room and began to rummage through her dresser drawers. Winters were cold in Iowa, and Mother had several pairs of sensible cotton and wool anklets, but none of them seemed big enough. We could barely fit one small bowl into each sock. My sister lifted out a cardboard packet. "What about these?" she said. We looked at each other, than at the beige nylon stockings, never worn, folded neatly around the cardboard. Mother didn't have many nylons; this was just a few years after the war and they were still expensive. But we knew these stockings would be big enough to hold our dishes. "I think if we're careful, it'll be okay," I said.

We tiptoed out of the bedroom with the nylons hidden under my sister's skirt.

Early Christmas morning we crept quietly out of our beds, scarcely breathing as we passed Mother's door, desperately hoping she wouldn't hear our feet on the creaky wooden stairs. In the living room we hurriedly stuffed her stockings, using both nylons, yanking them wide to accommodate the jagged edges of the cut-glass bowls. We didn't try to hang them up. They were too heavy. Instead we propped them against the bureau that we used for Santa in the absence of a fireplace. Then we looked at the bulging stockings, grinned with pleasure at each other and ran to call Mother.

When she sleepily entered the living room, her eyes were immediately riveted to the bureau. Two green cut-glass bowls hung precariously over the tops of her stretched, snagged, new nylon stockings. "My!" she said "Did you girls do all this?" There was something odd in her tone, but she quickly recovered. "What absolutely beautiful bowls!" she said admiringly, sitting down on the floor and taking them out one by one, setting them in a row on the floor for us all to enjoy. She hugged us both. We were so proud we had pleased her. "You are wonderful girls to have thought of this, and I love you both very much," she said. She ignored the empty stockings on the floor beside her.

Now a mother myself, living alone with a nine-year-old daughter, at Christmas I think of many things, but always I remember that Christmas of the cut-glass bowls. To me it shines as a beacon my mother has left me, a beacon to guide me through the maze of conflicting feelings, emotional demands, free-floating guilt and worry that afflct me at that time of year. When my mother looked at those ruined stockings and ugly cut-glass bowls, which eventually disappeared into the deep recesses of her bottom shelves, she knew what Christmas was all about. "I love you both very much."

It is often hard for me to remember what Christmas is all about. As a teacher on the semester plan, I always find myself buried under term papers and final examinations just before Christmas, a weight that may not be lifted until New Year's, when grades are irrevocably due. Meanwhile a mountain of mail begins to build up on my dining-room table, from aunts, cousins, dear old friends, all of whom need to hear from me. I have presents to wrap hurriedly at the last minute.

My daughter has a sudden desperate desire to make things. The tree needs to be planted firmly in its stand, lighted, decorated; where are the candles that always go on the mantle? Marking a paper with red pencil, trying to stay within the margins and be helpful but not unkind, I throw it down on the floor when the phone rings. Can we come to Sunday brunch across town? Will I bring a salad? I have no time at Christmas, no time at all.

So I try to think of the cut-glass bowls. I put Christmas carols on the hi-fi ("Play 'Rudolph, the Red-Nosed Reindeer' again, Mommy") and sit down to examine my own priorities. What do I want out of Christmas? What does it mean to me at the heart of the rustling tissue paper, blinking lights, ringing telephone? What must I find time to do? As I listen to the familiar carols my mind begins to clear. I realize first that Christmas means, oddly enough, silence. At Christmas I feel more than ever a need to get away from myself, from others, and listen to the quiet. I find myself taking long walks after dark, walking by my neighbors' houses, looking at their trees blazing in the windows, admiring the cheerful displays on their outdoor evergreens. I listen to the crackle of frosty branches in the wind, the crunch of my footsteps on the ice, my own moist breath as I puff into a wool scarf that holds a faint scent of mothballs.

On a cold, bright night when the stars are out above the city and the remaining elms on our street cast strange, dark patterns on the white snow, it seems to me while I walk that I can listen to time passing. I can almost hear the year slipping by. I always feel a little sad, recalling past losses and failures, but then I think of what we celebrate at Christmas, a birth and a new beginning, and I am comforted. I can feel hope in the air and see it sparkle in the lighted trees. I have another chance. Next year maybe I will do better.

Sometimes during Christmas week, I promise myself, I will find a small family church where I can listen to the simple words of the King James version of the Nativity, with their promise and joy. I will see a straw crèche, sing "Silent Night" and "It Came Upon the Midnight Clear," light a small candle myself and hold it briefly aloft, a token of continuing faith that somehow, somewhere, all will be well.

Walking down my street at night, I let my mind wander over the past. There I always meet old friends and invent conversations with them, trying to imagine what they look like now, asking them how they're doing. That is why I use Christmas as a time to restore damaged or dying relationships. During the holidays I recklessly run up my phone bill to call distant friends

I'm worried about. What is Joyce doing in Richmond? Is Sally lonely this Christmas in London? Why haven't I heard from Linda in Vancouver? Has Larry recovered from his mother's death? I once startled an old lover by calling him after four years at Christmas to ask how he was, how the children were, did they visit often, was he happy. That call laid an unhappy ghost finally and completely to rest.

Then for weeks during January I answer my cards, glue snapshots of my daughter on top of printed messages, write short letters, ask a few questions that may not be answered until next Christmas, when the cards come again. One year my favorite Christmas card read simply, "Of all things this coming year, be careful of love." At Christmas I try to keep the small flames glowing on candles that may be burning out for want of care.

Perhaps as part of my wish to reaffirm bonds at Christmas, I also make some time to spend in my kitchen, baking special treats to share with others. I study glossy pictures in magazines, clip recipes, read them to myself at night in bed. If I didn't have a full-time job, I fantasize, I could spend the whole month creating gingerbread houses, turning out dozens of decorated cookies, rushing from door to door with loaves of swirled, candied, beraisined bread. As it is, I usually have to settle for one long Saturday morning surrounded by spotted, yellowing recipes never used; cake flour that seems a suspicious antique gray; fancy molds dug out from cobwebbed corners. Last year it was plum pudding, from scratch, with as many jeweled fruits as I could stuff into the batter — three plum puddings, actually, since my molds all were rather small. We ate one Christmas Day, gave one to friends to take home, shared another with neighbors later in the week. For days after the actual baking smells were gone, an aroma of warmth and sweetness seemed to linger in my kitchen.

I am always tired after Christmas. Sometimes I get cranky, catch cold, come down with a headache — signs of stress, I do not need to be told. It may be foolish to try to cram so much into an already bursting schedule, to sandwich concerts around exams to be graded, plum pudding between cards to be answered, a long walk under starlight when presents are waiting to be wrapped. But I cannot bring myself to give up any more of Christmas than I am absolutely forced to. I fervently pack it all in as my sister and I stuffed those glass dishes into Mother's stretching nylons so many Christmases ago. Like my mother, I want to set out the tokens of love on the living-room floor, look past their gaudy color and cut-glass gleam, ignore the ruined stockings that held them and remember why they are there.

—Ted Daniels